I.   Overview Analysis of Achievements and Challenges Since 1995

A.   Achievements

In recent decades, women's participation in the workforce has transformed the American economy. Today, nearly half of all primary breadwinners are women, and since 1970, women's labor has contributed $13,000 to the median family income and expanded the economy by $2 trillion dollars. Young women today are also more likely than young men to graduate college, and just as likely to earn advanced degrees. Yet, despite these gains, women still earn just 78 cents for every dollar men earn, and women of color earn even less making it more difficult to provide for their families and secure the promise of the American dream. Women also experience unacceptably high levels of violence, from domestic abuse to sexual assault, and gender disparities persist in health care access and workplace policies.

From his earliest days in office, President Obama has worked to address these issues by combatting discrimination, expanding access to health care, supporting women-owned businesses and taking action to keep women safe from violence at home and in school. In addition, from creating the White House Council on Women and Girls to appointing two women to the Supreme Court and a strong team of women leaders to his Cabinet and White House staff, President Obama has taken concrete steps to ensure that women are involved in shaping every level of our government and that their voices are heard throughout society and all around the world.

Building on this commitment to supporting and fighting for women and working families, the President has made 2014 a Year of Action, focused on expanding opportunity for all Americans. A key part of this agenda is pursuing policies that help women succeed, recognizing the critical and growing contributions they make to our economy and its continued recovery. We know that when women succeed, America succeeds and the President will continue to use all of the tools at his disposal – working with members of Congress where they are willing, acting on his own where they aren't, and partnering with business leaders, governors, mayors and other stakeholders – to take action on behalf of women, girls and their families.

Specific examples of the President's commitment include improved laws, both statutory and regulatory, for women; increased emphasis on women and girls in foreign policy; and new institutional mechanisms to advance gender equality.

Improved Laws for Women

Ensuring Quality, Affordable Health Care for Women and Girls. The Affordable Care Act (ACA) ensures that every American can access high-quality, affordable coverage, providing health insurance to millions of Americans who would otherwise be uninsured. Efficiently and effectively implementing the ACA is one of the Administration's highest priorities. Women have already benefitted from the ACA; no longer can women be charged more for insurance just because of their gender or for preexisting conditions, and women are now receiving preventive care, including contraception, without copays, co-insurance or deductibles. Now many plans must cover maternity and prenatal care. Finally, as of this year, millions of women and families across the country enrolled in either private insurance through the Health Insurance Marketplace or for coverage through Medicaid. Americans have the security of knowing that if they want to change jobs or start their own business, they will have access to affordable health insurance for their family.

The Violence Against Women Act (VAWA). On March 7, 2013, President Obama signed the Violence Against Women Reauthorization Act (VAWA) of 2013, which maintains programs that reduce domestic and sexual violence and expands and improves the Federal government's response to violence against women. VAWA 2013 includes provisions that support the sovereignty of American Indian and Alaska Native tribes to hold perpetrators accountable – a necessary step to reducing violence against Native women. The reauthorization of VAWA also ensures that lesbian, gay, bisexual and transgender survivors have access to the services they need and deserve; enables victims in publicly subsidized housing to stay safe by transferring to a different unit or location; and adds protections for college students, who experience high rates of rape and sexual assault . Altogether, VAWA funds more than $400 million each year, administered by the Office on Violence Against Women, to reduce domestic violence and sexual assault.

Signing Landmark Pay Discrimination Legislation. The very first piece of legislation President Obama signed into law was the Lilly Ledbetter Fair Pay Restoration Act of 2009. The Act reverses the Supreme Court's decision that the statute of limitations for pay discrimination claims starts at the date of the first discriminatory pay check. It also reinstates the long-standing interpretation of the law that treats each paycheck as a separate discriminatory act that starts a new clock for purposes of calculating the relevant statute of limitation. As a result, many women who have been discriminated against can now have their day in court to seek the pay they deserve. In addition, President Obama signed two Executive Actions on Equal Pay Day this year. On April 8, the President signed an Executive Order prohibiting federal contractors from retaliating against employees who choose to discuss their compensation, as well as a Presidential Memorandum instructing the Secretary of Labor to establish new regulations requiring federal contractors to submit to the Department of Labor summary data on compensation paid to their employees. The President also continues to advocate for the passage of the Paycheck Fairness Act, common sense legislation that would give women the tools they need to fight pay discrimination.

Increasing Emphasis on Women and Girls in Foreign Policy

Advancing Women's Economic Empowerment. The United States is leading new efforts in a range of multilateral forums to advance women's economic empowerment and help spur economic growth worldwide, from brokering new commitments to increase female labor force participation in the G20 to increasing women's entrepreneurship in the Asia Pacific Economic Cooperation (APEC) forum. The Administration has launched several signature regional programs to drive reforms and investments, including the APEC Women and the Economy initiative, the Women's Entrepreneurship in the Americas (WEAmericas) initiative, and the African Women's Entrepreneurship Program (AWEP). In 2009, the Administration launched the Feed the Future initiative to advance food security worldwide, with a priority focus on women agricultural producers as critical drivers of economic growth.

Promoting the Health of Women and Families. President Obama has placed women, girls, and gender equality at the heart of his global health agenda, including through the Global Health Initiative (GHI). The President's Emergency Plan for AIDS Relief (PEPFAR) has ensured a comprehensive approach to gender issues in HIV prevention, treatment, and care, including working to provide access to life-long anti-retroviral treatment for both mothers and their children. In January 2009, President Obama rescinded the Mexico City Policy which denied federal funds to health care and aid organizations that used non-U.S. government funding to perform or offer information about abortion services. The United States Agency for International Development (USAID) advances and supports voluntary family planning programs in more than 45 countries across the globe. In FY 2013 for example, USAID's family planning programs reached more than 84 million women and averted 21 million unintended pregnancies, preventing 15,000 maternal deaths and saving the lives of more than 230,000 infants. The U.S. Government has also restored funding to the UN Population Fund (UNFPA), providing over $200 million in funding since 2009 to the largest multilateral provider of family planning and reproductive health information and services with programs in 150 countries.

Empowering Women as Equal Partners in Preventing Conflict and Building Peace. On December 19, 2011, the Obama Administration released Executive Order 13595 and the U.S. National Action Plan on Women, Peace, and Security to support women's voices and perspectives in decision-making in countries threatened and affected by war, violence, and insecurity. Policies and programs work to strengthen prospects for peace and security through the empowerment and protection from violence of women and girls in countries affected by crisis, insecurity, and political transition. As part of this effort, the U.S. launched the Safe from the Start initiative in 2013 to better address the needs of women and girls and other groups at risk of Gender-Based Violence (GBV) in emergencies.

Addressing Gender-based Violence. On August 10, 2012, President Obama issued Executive Order 13623 directing departments and agencies to implement the first ever United States Strategy to Prevent and Respond to Gender-based Violence Globally. The Department of State and USAID have led the United States' work to prevent and respond to gender-based violence by ensuring that this issue is integrated in diplomacy and development efforts.

Creating a New Multilateral Partnership on Women's Political and Economic Participation. The Administration launched the Equal Futures Partnership in September 2012, which brings together partner countries from around the world to break down barriers to women's political and economic empowerment in their countries through legal, regulatory and policy reforms. U.S. commitments to the partnership have focused on supporting women entrepreneurs and civic education and leadership development for women and girls.

Established New Institutional Mechanisms to Advance Gender Equality

Establishing the White House Council on Women and Girls. On March 11, 2009, President Obama signed an Executive Order creating the White House Council on Women and Girls (CWG). CWG is comprised of representatives from each Federal agency, as well as the White House offices, and coordinates efforts across Federal agencies and departments to ensure that the needs of women and girls are taken into account in all programs, policies, and legislation. To aid in implementation of the CWG's mission, the President has created a number of positions, such as the first-ever White House Advisor on Violence Against Women and a Director for Human Rights and Gender in the White House National Security Council staff.

Creating an Ambassador-at-Large for Global Women's Issues. In 2013, President Obama signed a Presidential Memorandum that will help ensure that advancing the rights of women and girls remains central to U.S. diplomacy and development around the world - and that these efforts will continue to be led by public servants at the highest levels of the United States government. After appointing the United States' first-ever Ambassador-at-Large for Global Women's Issues at the beginning of his Administration, the Presidential Memorandum ensures that the Ambassador-at-Large reporting directly to the Secretary heads the State Department's Office of Global Women's Issues.

B. Challenges/Setbacks

Despite enormous progress in educational and employment attainment, American women still face significant inequities in wages and in health and safety outcomes. Women still earn 78 cents for every dollar men earn in the workplace, and women of color make even less. This challenge significantly impacts women trying to provide for their families and ensure a better future for their children, especially when women are forty percent of primary breadwinners. Furthermore, The United States is the only industrialized nation –and one of only several nations in the entire world – without some kind of paid parental leave. The face of the American family and the American worker has changed drastically over the past half century, but unfortunately our workplace policies – from lack of leave to lack of flexibility – have not kept pace. Violence, sexual assault, and domestic abuse also persist as significant challenges for women despite many positive achievements to prevent and respond to such violence. On college campuses one in five women are sexually assaulted, and minority and young women face the highest rates of domestic violence and sexual assault. And despite historic gains for women in reproductive health care, at the state level and at the Supreme Court, rights are being rolled back and dismantled.

Furthermore, the United States is one of seven countries that has not ratified the Convention of the Elimination of All Forms of Discrimination Against Women, commonly known as CEDAW or the Women's Treaty. Administration officials have testified to Congress in support of ratification of the treaty, noting that doing so would send a powerful message about our commitment to equality for women around the world lend much-needed validation and support to advocates fighting against the oppression of women and girls everywhere.

Addressing these challenges is limited by a range of factors. Such obstacles include lack of political will to pass essential legislation, women's limited representation in leadership positions in Congress and business, and discriminatory gender norms in organizations. Women's under representation and negative representation in the media also represent major challenges and reinforce existing gender bias.

The Administration continues to address the economic, political and social barriers that women and girls face in the United States and in countries across the world. Though convening power, regulatory changes, Executive Orders and Presidential Memorandums, President Obama has tackled the major challenges and setbacks that women face, head on.

C.   Constitutional, Legislative, and Legal Developments

The main legislative developments include the Affordable Care Act, the Reauthorization of the Violence Against Women Act, the Lilly Ledbetter Fair Pay Restoration Act of 2009, and other worker and business protection rules from the Department of Labor and other Federal government agencies (see the achievements section for additional detail).

D.   National Budget

The President's Budget is developed to support the priorities of the Administration and the needs of the American people. Many programs and policies work to advance gender equality, though program budgets year to year are not directly based off of any specific gender equality targets. The Fiscal Year 2015 Budget takes a number of steps to create opportunity for women and girls, including:

Promoting Equal Pay for Equal Work. The Budget makes important investments to help ensure that women receive equal pay for equal work. It provides additional resources to strengthen the pay discrimination enforcement efforts of the Department of Labor's Office of Federal Contract Compliance Programs and maintains strong support for the Equal Employment Opportunity Commission, agencies that work to secure equal employment opportunities for all workers.

Encouraging State Paid Leave Initiatives. Too many American workers must make the painful choice between the care of their families and a paycheck they desperately need. While the Family and Medical Leave Act allows many workers to take job-protected unpaid time off, millions of families cannot afford to use unpaid leave. A handful of States have enacted policies to offer paid leave, but more States should have the chance to follow their example. The President's budget requested a $105 million to provide technical assistance and support to States that are considering paid leave programs.

Raising the Minimum Wage to $10.10. Over the past 30 years, modest minimum wage increases have not kept pace with the higher costs of basic necessities for working families. No one who works full time should have to raise his or her family in poverty. In 2014, President Obama signed an Executive Order raising the minimum wage to $10.10 for workers on new federal contracts. He also called on Congress to raise the minimum wage for all workers to $10.10, and index this wage to the cost of living. The President's plan would benefit around 28 million workers. More than half of all workers who would benefit from increasing the minimum wage to $10.10 are women. Since the President called on Congress to act in his 2013 State of the Union address, 13 states and the District of Columbia have increased their own minimum wages.

Continuing Efforts to Combat Violence Against Women. The President's proposed 2015 Budget provides $423 million to reinforce efforts to fund programs under the Violence Against Women Act. As a result of prior investments in this area, civil and criminal justice systems are more responsive to victims, and crimes of violence committed against women have declined in recent years. Yet, reducing such violence and meeting the needs of the almost 1.3 million women victimized by rape and sexual assault annually, and the nearly seven million victims of intimate partner violence each year, remains a critical priority. This funding includes $193 million for STOP Grants to Combat Violence Against Women, $27 million for the Sexual Assault Services Program (SASP), and $11 million to reduce violent crimes against women on college campuses. The Budget also provides $35 million for a new grant program for communities to develop coordinated teams to address their untested sexual assault kits at law enforcement agencies or backlogged at crime labs. These grants will bring law enforcement agencies, prosecutors, victim, advocates, and crime labs together to address the problem.

Supporting Victims of Domestic Violence and Human Trafficking. The Budget provides $140 million for shelters, supportive services, and a national hotline for victims of domestic violence. The Budget also includes $10 million for a Department of Health and Human Services (HHS) initiative to prevent and address domestic human trafficking in addition to anti-trafficking efforts by the Departments of Justice and Homeland Security. This initiative will provide direct services to domestic victims of trafficking, train service providers, and invest in data collection, research, and evaluation.

Renewing Efforts to Promote Juvenile Justice and Fight Youth Violence. The Budget proposes $299 million for the Department of Justice's Juvenile Justice Programs and includes evidence-based investments to prevent youth violence. These investments include $18 million to fund the Community-Based Violence Prevention Initiative and $4 million for the National Forum on Youth Violence Prevention. Further, the Budget makes available $23 million for research and pilot projects focused on developing appropriate responses for youth exposed to violence.

Enhancing Access to High-Quality Early Childhood Education. To build a foundation for success in the formative early years of life, the Budget increases access to high-quality early childhood education.

- Supports a Preschool for All initiative, in partnership with the States, to provide all low- and moderate-income four-year-olds with access to high-quality preschool, while encouraging States to expand those programs to reach additional children from middle-class families and establish full-day kindergarten policies.
- Extends and expands evidence-based, voluntary home visiting programs, which enable nurses, social workers, and other professionals to connect families to services to support the child's health, development, and ability to learn.

- Pays for these initiatives by raising Federal tobacco taxes, which will also help discourage youth smoking and save lives.
- Provides access to high-quality infant and toddler care to a total of more than 100,000 children through Early Head Start-Child Care Partnerships, and supports Head Start grantees who are expanding program duration and investing in teacher quality.
- Makes a substantial commitment to both maintain the number of children served by the Child Care Development Fund and improve the quality of care, with sufficient mandatory funding to support more than 1.4 million children for a full ten years while investing in significant quality improvements.

Expanding the Child and Dependent Care Tax Credit for Children Under Age Five. In recognition of the higher costs of high quality day care for infants and small children, the Budget proposes to expand the Child and Dependent Care Tax Credit tax credit. In addition to the current credit, taxpayers with up to two children under age five would be eligible for an additional credit on total expenses up to $4,000 per child.

Preventing Teen Pregnancy. The Budget continues funding for evidence-based models that prevent teenage pregnancy to build on the significant progress that has been made in this area.

Ensuring Quality, Affordable Health Care for Women and Girls. The Affordable Care Act (ACA) ensures that every American can access high-quality, affordable coverage, providing health insurance to millions of Americans who would otherwise be uninsured. Efficiently and effectively implementing the ACA is one of the Administration's highest priorities. Women have already benefitted from the ACA; no longer can women be charged more for insurance just because of their gender or for preexisting conditions, and women are now receiving preventive care without copays, co-insurance or deductibles. Finally, as of this year, millions of women and families across the country enrolled in either private insurance through the Health Insurance Marketplace or for coverage through Medicaid. Americans have the security of knowing that if they want to change jobs or start their own business, they will have access to health insurance for their family. Additionally, premium tax credits and cost sharing assistance are making coverage affordable.

Supporting Women-Owned Businesses. The Budget includes Small Business Administration funding to support the operations of more than 100 Women's Business Centers. These centers annually provide counseling and training to more than 120,000 women entrepreneurs looking to expand or start small businesses. In addition, the Budget continues support for the Women's Business Council to serve as an independent source of advice and policy recommendations on issues of economic importance to women business owners.

Ensuring Workers Receive the Pay and Overtime They Earned. The Budget proposes an increase of more than $41 million for the Department of Labor's Wage and Hour Division to increase enforcement of the laws that ensure that workers receive appropriate wages and overtime pay, as well as the right to take job-protected leave for family and medical purposes. This would allow the Wage and Hour Division will be able to hire 300 new investigators across the country to help in this effort, and using risk-based approaches to target the industries and employers most likely to break the law.

Expanding the EITC for Childless Workers. Few things help families with children pull themselves up through hard work like the Earned Income Tax Credit (EITC). However, the maximum EITC available to childless workers, including non-custodial parents, is only $500, and the credit is unavailable to workers under age 25, which means that it cannot shape work decisions during the crucial years at the beginning of a young person's career. The Budget doubles the maximum credit to $1,000, makes the credit available to workers at slightly higher income levels (e.g. a full-time minimum wage worker at the current minimum wage), and lowers the age limit from 25 to 21, as a way to support and reward work. The proposal also updates the childless worker EITC upper age limit for increases in the Social Security Normal Retirement Age (raising it from 64 to 66). The proposed EITC expansion will benefit 13.5 million workers, including 6.1 million women. These changes will be paid for by closing high-income tax loopholes.

Supporting Affordable Rental Housing for 4.5 Million Families. The Budget includes $20 billion for the Housing Choice Voucher program ($0.9 billion more than the 2014 enacted level) to help more than 2.2 million low-income families afford decent housing in neighborhoods of their choice. This funding level not only supports all existing vouchers, but restores reductions in assisted housing units that resulted from the 2013 sequestration funding cut and provides an additional 40,000 new vouchers including 10,000 for homeless veterans. The Budget also includes $9.7 billion for the Project-Based Rental Assistance program to maintain affordable rental housing for 1.2 million families. Further, the Budget provides $6.5 billion in operating and capital subsidies to preserve affordable public housing for 1.1 million families, an increase of $0.3 billion over the 2014 enacted level. Together, HUD's core rental assistance programs serve 4.5 million households, more than 75 percent of which are headed by females. An additional $10 million for the Rental Assistance Demonstration (RAD) will be targeted to public housing properties in high-poverty neighborhoods, including designated Promise Zones, where the Administration is also supporting comprehensive revitalization efforts. RAD leverages private financing to reduce backlogs of capital repairs and the Budget proposes to eliminate the cap on the number of units eligible for this demonstration.

Continuing Progress Toward Ending Homelessness. The Budget provides $2.4 billion for the Department of Housing and Urban Development's Homeless Assistance Grants, $301 million above the 2014 enacted level. This funding supports new permanent supportive housing units and maintains more than 330,000 HUD-funded beds that assist the homeless nationwide. Through this investment as well as collaborative partnerships with local governments, non-profit organizations, and among Federal agencies, the Administration will continue to make progress towards the President's ambitious goals to end homelessness across the country, including the goal to prevent and end homelessness for families, youth, and children by 2020.

Supporting Nutrition for Women, Children and Infants. The Budget provides $6.8 billion to support the 8.7 million individuals expected to participate in the Special Supplemental Nutrition Program for Women, Infants, and Children (WIC), which is critical to the health of pregnant women, new mothers, infants, and young children. The Budget also supports changes to the food package that will improve consumption of nutritious foods that are important to healthy child development.

E.   **Mechanisms for Dialogue with Civil Society**

In the United States, all citizens and civil society organizations can have a direct influence on policy by communicating with their representatives, and they have a variety of means at their disposal to do so. Individuals and groups can request personal meetings with Senators and Representatives in their local offices or their Washington offices. They may initiate communications by telephone, email or letter: as a rule, in most U.S. congressional offices, all letters from constituents receive a response, and nearly all phone calls from constituents are returned, generally a staff member may respond on behalf of the member. They can also share information and gather feedback from constituents through grassroots letter writing campaigns and at public gatherings or town halls that are advertised through public notices or mailings.

All external stakeholders including civil society organizations, women's organizations, academia, faith-based organizations, the private sector, and other actors, can communicate directly with staff at Federal Agencies and The White House. Specifically, stakeholders and members of the general public can contact the White House through the White House Office of Public Engagement (OPE). OPE serves as the "front door" of the White House, and can be reached by phone and e-mail. Members of the public can also petition The White House through an initiative called "We The People," which can be found at www.petitions.whitehouse.gov.

F.   Cooperation to Share Knowledge and Experiences

Within the U.S. government, there are a number of key coordination mechanisms that are in place in order to ensure that Federal departments and agencies advance the interests of women and girls in policy, programs, and legislation.

- At the White House Council on Women and Girls (CWG), meetings and policy processes occur at all levels with varying frequency. Meetings include representatives from Federal agencies as well as the White House Office. The Council on Women and Girls coordinates efforts among federal agencies and White House policy councils, including the National Economic Council, the Domestic Policy Council, and the National Security Council.

- CWG has created a number of working groups on specific topics, to facilitate interagency coordination, including a working group on Violence Against Women, Women in STEM and Women Veterans.

- CWG coordinates messaging across agencies, including through email outreach, a weekly newsletter to the public, and blog posts.

- There also exist a number of Memorandums of Understanding (MOUs) for interagency cooperation, including, for example, the MOU between the Department of Labor, the Equal Employment Opportunity Commission, the Office of Personnel Management and the Department of Justice regarding pay equity.

The primary mechanism for coordinating relations between the Federal government and the states is through legislation or regulations. Communications and event outreach on specific issues areas also serves as an important coordination mechanism. The Administration highlights the important work that is getting done at the local level that represents the interests of women and girls and includes representatives from the state and local level at various events.

G.   Millennium Development Goals and Beijing Declaration

The Millennium Development Goals have complimented the Beijing Declaration and Platform for Action, and together have bolstered the United States' investments in ensuring women and girls' access to services and opportunities across a wide range of sectors, from health, to education, to employment. These platforms have informed both policy and strategic vision for priority areas.

II. Progress in the Implementation of the Critical Areas of Concern since 2009

A. Women and Poverty

1) Domestic Efforts

(a) <u>Revised Laws to Ensure Women's Equal Rights and Access to Economic Resources</u>

Fighting Pay Discrimination. The first piece of legislation President Obama signed into law was the Lilly Ledbetter Fair Pay Act, which restored basic protections against pay discrimination. The President continues to advocate for the passage of the Paycheck Fairness Act, which is common sense legislation that gives women the tools they need to fight pay discrimination. And President Obama has convened an Equal Pay Task Force to ensure that existing equal pay laws are fully enforced. Through this Task Force, key agencies in the Federal government are coordinating and enhancing their efforts to protect women from pay discrimination.

Ensuring Fair Labor Standards for In-Home Care Workers. Fulfilling a promise by the President to ensure that home care workers receive a fair day's pay for a fair day's work, The Department of Labor (DOL) issued a final rule ensuring that the Fair Labor Standards Act's minimum wage and overtime protections apply to most of the nation's workers who provide essential home and personal care assistance to elderly people and people with disabilities. These occupations are projected to experience substantial growth in the coming years. Yet despite this projected growth, workers in these fields are among the lowest paid workers, and of the nearly two million workers who will be affected by this rule, approximately 90 percent are women. These home health aides, personal care aides, and certified nursing assistants who provide home and personal care services will receive the same basic protections already provided to most U.S. workers. The rule will also help guarantee that those who rely on the assistance of direct care workers have access to an increasingly professional workforce.

Preventing and Ending Homelessness for Women. According to a report from the Department of Housing and Urban Development, 77.9% of sheltered homeless people in families in 2012 were women, down from 82% in 2007. Thanks to the Homelessness Prevention and Rapid Re-housing Program, passed as part of President Obama's American Recovery and Investment Act (ARRA), an estimated 700,000 women have been saved from homelessness since the beginning of this Administration.

(b) <u>Other</u>

Giving Working Families a Raise. In 2014, President Obama signed an Executive Order raising the minimum wage to $10.10 for workers on new federal contracts. He also called on Congress to raise the minimum wage for all workers to $10.10, and index this wage to the cost of living. The President's plan would benefit around 28 million workers. More than half of all workers who would benefit from increasing the minimum wage to $10.10 are women. Since the President called on Congress to act in his 2013 State of the Union address, 13 states and the District of Columbia have increased their own minimum wages.

Tax Credits for Working Families. Existing research shows that refundable tax credits conditional on employment substantially increase labor force participation, particularly among single mothers. Researchers credit expansions of the EITC in the 1980s and 1990s with substantial increases in labor force participation among single mothers, in fact, EITC expansions account for more than half of the increase in employment among single mothers during this time period. Early in his Administration, the President pushed for significant improvements to tax credits for working families, which Congress extended on a bipartisan basis through 2017. These improvements include expansions to the Earned

Income Tax Credit (EITC) and Child Tax Credit, which strengthen work incentives and help parents afford the costs of raising a family, and the creation of the American Opportunity Tax Credit, which helps working and middle-class families pay for college. Together, these improvements provide an average of more than $1,000 in tax relief to 26 million families every year. The President's Budget proposes to make these improvements permanent, while doing even more to promote work and support families through improving tax credits that help families with young children afford the rising costs of child care, and expanding the EITC for workers without children and non-custodial parents, including by making it available to younger workers.

Ensuring Access to Unemployment Insurance for 1.8 Million Women in 2013. Unemployment benefits provide income support for all members of the households in which recipients live. Since 2009, more than 22 million laid-off workers have received federal Unemployment Insurance benefits, of which almost 9 million are women. In 2013, unemployment insurance kept 1.2 million people out of poverty. In 2013, up to 1.8 million women were eligible for unemployment insurance under the EUC program. Unemployment in the U.S. has come down significantly since 2009, but the recovery has been somewhat slower for women, and there is still work to do. The Administration supports re-instating the Federal extension of unemployment benefits until more workers are back on the job, which would provide support to the estimated 4.1 percent of households where an adult female earner is unemployed.

Improving Access to Unemployment Insurance. The American Recovery and Reinvestment Act of 2009 (ARRA) made $7 billion in incentive payments available to states to encourage them to reform their UI programs. For instance, it provided incentives for states to allow workers to collect UI after voluntarily leaving a job for "compelling domestic circumstances" like caring for a sick child, partner, or parent, or to escape domestic violence or stalking. To date, 20 states have adopted this change, guaranteeing women workers in their jurisdictions temporary income support when they have to make a hard choice between their families or safety and their work. Likewise, 28 states made changes to allow those seeking part-time work to receive UI, which is particularly beneficial to women who are more likely to be part-time workers.

Fighting Lending Discrimination Against Women. In 2013, The Department of Housing and Urban Development (HUD) continued to aggressively investigate and resolve cases where women experienced lending discrimination because they were pregnant or on parental leave. HUD settled a total of 28 cases in 2013, obtaining almost $300,000 for 43 complainants. As a result of these investigations, some of the country's largest lenders have changed their policies and practices on maternity leave lending decision making, and Fannie Mae and Freddie Mac have updated their mortgage guidelines to remove unnecessary lending barriers to women on parental leave.

Working to Re-integrate Formerly Incarcerated Women. In 2012, DOL awarded nearly $32 million in grants to community-based organizations that will provide job training, education and support services to formerly incarcerated youth and women as they make the transition back to their communities. The goal of these grants is to provide employment-focused services and support to help participants overcome traumas like physical and sexual abuse, family turmoil, mental health and substance abuse and other barriers to successful reintegration to society. In addition, HUD is a member of the Federal Interagency Reentry Council Women and Reentry Workgroup which has created a strategic approach to focusing on the needs of incarcerated and returning women. HUD, in collaboration with the Office of National Drug Control Policy (ONDCP), has drafted their first series of reports profiling successful housing and reentry successful efforts.

2) Efforts Abroad

(a) Development Strategies

Promoting Women's Rights across Development Investments. Gender equality and female empowerment are fundamental to the realization of the human rights of women and key to effective and sustainable development outcomes. Although many gender gaps have narrowed over the past two decades, substantial inequalities remain across every development priority worldwide – from political participation to economic inclusion – particularly in low-income and conflict-affected countries and among disadvantaged groups. United States' investments seek to reduce gender disparities in access to, control over and benefit from resources, wealth, opportunities and services - economic, social, political, and cultural; reduce gender-based violence and mitigate its harmful effects on individuals; and increase capability of women and girls to realize their rights, determine their life outcomes, and influence decision-making in households, communities, and societies. For example, to better enable women agricultural producers to reach their full potential, the Administration launched the Feed the Future initiative in 2009. Feed the Future promotes women's leadership in agriculture, fosters policy changes that increase women's land ownership and strengthens their access to financial services, encourages female farmers to adopt new agricultural technology aimed at increasing productivity and reducing unpaid work, and invests in improved nutrition outcomes. The New Alliance for Food Security and Nutrition, launched at the Camp David G-8 Summit, invests in smallholder farmers, particularly **women, who play a critical role in transforming agriculture and building thriving economies.**

(b) Promoting Economic Opportunities

A range of departments and agencies working overseas invest in promoting women's access to economic opportunities. The U.S. has created and expanded regional programs to provide women business owners around the world with access to the skills, networks, and financing they need to expand their businesses and become greater forces for economic progress. U.S. support of women entrepreneurs is described below in Section F on economic empowerment and additional efforts to promote women's political and economic empowerment, including through the Equal Futures Partnership, are described below in Section G. In addition to broad investments by State and USAID, the Overseas Private Investment Corporation (OPIC) works to expand economic opportunities for women, including through extensive support for microfinance and by providing incentives for banks to lend to female entrepreneurs in places such as Cambodia, Egypt and Turkey. The Treasury Department has been supporting efforts to identify and expand financial access to women—especially women entrepreneurs—through innovative lending models such as partnerships and direct support to international finance institutions, including the Inter-American Development Bank. The Treasury Department is also supporting the G20 Global Partnership on Financial Inclusion (GPFI) to address barriers to women's financial inclusion. GPFI is working on policy recommendations and legal system reforms within the G20 countries to increase women's financial literacy and financial inclusion.

B. Education and Training of Women

1) Domestic Efforts

(a) Early Childhood Education

Making Historic Investments to Expand Access to High-Quality Child Care and Early Education. The President has prioritized continuous improvement of the Head Start program, which serves nearly one million children from birth to age 5 each year. Through the Recovery Act, the President and

Congress took important steps to expand Head Start and Early Head Start by adding more than 64,000 slots for these programs. ARRA investments in the Child Care and Development Fund also increased access to child care for an additional 300,000 children and families. In his 2013 State of the Union address, President Obama called on Congress to expand access to high-quality preschool for every child in America, and established a comprehensive early education agenda with a series of new investments to establish a continuum of high-quality early learning for a child—beginning at birth and continuing to age 5. In 2014, the Department of Health and Human Services began this work with a $500 million competitive grant opportunity to support the expansion of Early Head Start and the creation of Early Head Start-Child Care Partnerships and the Department of Education announced a $250 million Preschool Development Grants competition to enhance state preschool programs and expand access to high-quality preschool for four-year-olds in high-need communities to model the President's Preschool for All vision.

Promoting Access to Child Care for Workers in Job Training Programs. DOL will make funds available for technical skill training grants to provide low-wage individuals opportunities to advance in their careers in in-demand industries, with $25 million of the competition focused on addressing barriers to training faced by those with childcare responsibilities. With the help of additional public or private funding that it will leverage, these dedicated funds will promote greater availability of activities such as co-location of training and child care services, access to unconventional training delivery times or locations, flexibilities related to scheduling and child care exigencies, and improved access to related child care services. These funds will give more working families a path to secure, higher wage jobs by addressing the significant barriers related to finding and acquiring affordable, high quality child care—including emergency care—while attending skills training programs. For example, evidence shows that single parents who receive child care are much more likely to complete job training programs than those who do not have access to child care. The new competition, which will be launched next year, will aim to increase participation and completion rates of those in training by supporting sustainable and innovative approaches that expand workers' access to child care.

Expanding Access to Home Visiting. The President has proposed a series of new investments that will establish a continuum of high-quality early learning for a child—beginning at birth and continuing to age 5 - including expanding evidence-based, voluntary home visits for parents and children. HHS will provide new grants in 2014 to serve additional at-risk families during pregnancy and children's early years through the Maternal, Infant, and Early Childhood Home Visiting Program. Through this program, states are implementing voluntary programs that provide nurses, social workers, and other professionals to meet with at-risk families in their homes and connect them to assistance that impacts a child's health, development, and ability to learn. These programs have been critical in improving maternal and child health outcomes in the early years, leaving long-lasting, positive impacts on parenting skills; children's cognitive, language, and social-emotional development; and school readiness.

(b) K-12 Education

Investing in School Improvement Grants. The Obama Administration has invested over $5 billion in all 50 states to transform America's lowest-performing schools through the School Improvement Grants program. This program has provided unprecedented levels of support - up to $6 million per school over three years - to transform the persistently lowest-performing schools into safe and effective learning environments, with some schools seeing double-digit increases in test scores and significant growth in high school graduation rates.

Supporting High School Redesign. The President has called on America's school districts and their community partners to use existing resources to transform the high school experience for America's youth through a whole school redesign effort. Schools are challenged to rethink the high school learning experience in ways that will benefit each student on an individual level through personalizing learning opportunities, providing academic and wrap-around support services, and providing career-related experiences or competencies for young women and men. In April 2014, the President announced a $107 million down payment to expand this vision to 24 communities across the country.

Creating Excellent Educators for All. Young women of every background deserve the best classroom role models possible, which is why the Department of Education will publish Educator Equity profiles in Fall 2014 to help states identify gaps in access to quality teaching for low-income and minority students. The Department is also investing $4.2 million to launch a new technical assistance network to support states and districts in developing and implementing their plans to ensure all students have access to great educators.

(c) Higher Education

Creating the $2,500 American Opportunity Tax Credit (AOTC). Nearly 12 million Americans will use the AOTC to help finance their postsecondary education next. Students and families can receive up to $10,000 in AOTC over 4 years to help pay for college.

Increasing the Maximum Pell Grant Award by $1,000. President Obama pushed to increase the maximum Pell grant award, which will rise to $5,730 in 2014-15. Over 5.8 million total women receive Pell grants or another federal scholarship, compared to over 3.5 million men

Keeping Student Loan Interest Rates Low. The President has also fought to ensure that student loan interest rates stay low to provide borrowers with income-based repayment options that will help the 580,309 women at community colleges accessing loans to pay for college (more than double the number since 2007-08). 38 percent of women take out federal loans, compared to 31 percent of men. The President directed the Secretary of Education to ensure that student loans remain affordable for all who borrowed federal direct loans as students by allowing them cap their payments at 10 percent of their monthly incomes. The Department of Education formally began its process to amend its regulations this fall with a goal of making the new plan available to borrowers by December 2015.

(d) Promoting Opportunities for Women in Science, Technology, Engineering, and Mathematics (STEM)

Attracting and Retaining Women and Girls in STEM. Building a pathway to high-paying, high-skilled jobs for women and girls, the Administration has featured competitive preference for inspiring and engaging girls in science, technology, engineering, and mathematics (STEM) through the President's $4.35 billion Race to the Top program, the 2013 Youth Career Connect grants to redesign high schools so that students complete prepared for college and career, and additional education reform programs. Federal agencies have deployed their STEM workforce and have partnered with the private sector to increase mentorship of girls and women in STEM, for example, by The Department of Energy (DOE) forming new partnerships with 100kin10 and US2020 to reach classrooms and mentors, respectively, with their Women @ Energy series profiling women in STEM careers to inspire the next generation of energy scientists and engineers. Supporting and retaining America's female scientists and engineers was a focus of the June 2014 White House Summit on Working Families at which NSF announced implementation nearly a year ahead of schedule of cost allowance policies for childcare at professional conferences that lesson the challenges for working families and NIH released a comprehensive summary of research on barriers and opportunities to attract and retain women in biomedical science careers and is using that evidence base to guide Administration policies to broaden participation and success of women in STEM fields.

President Obama and First Lady Michelle Obama Launched National Campaign to Great Response. College, Universities, and philanthropic partners have launched new programs, scholarships, and outreach, in response to the President and First Lady's call at the White House College Opportunity event in January 2014, to expand STEM college completion for more underserved students, including broadening achievement to women and minorities in STEM fields in which they are under-represented.

National Aeronautics and Space Administration (NASA) Reaches Students in Classrooms with Inspiration from Space. NASA's Digital Learning Network (DLN) brings NASA professionals together with students across the country through web conferencing tools enabling in-depth exploration of STEM topics. This year, DLN will host specific events that target women and girls, including events during Women's History Month 2014.

National Science Foundation (NSF) Invests in Research and Programs to Support Women and Girls Success in STEM Education and Careers. Supporting and retaining America's female scientists and engineers is the goal of the NSF ten-year "career-life balance initiative," launched at the White House in September 2011 to promote flexibility for researchers who wish to work and care for families. With these and other family friendly policies, Federal science research agencies are stepping up to reduce the false choice faced by women and men entering research careers of starting a family or continuing on a trajectory to productive faculty research positions. In 2013, NSF held the third Gender Summit, convening women from all over the world to discuss ways to improve the achievement of women and girls in STEM education and careers. NSF is reaching out to researchers across a number of existing NSF research, development and workforce programs to encourage submissions of proposals focused on advancing women and girls in STEM education.

Mobilizing Federal STEM Employees to Mentor and Teach in STEM. To mobilize the 200,000 Federal STEM employees to volunteer in STEM-related activities and inspire students and, in particular, young girls, by providing STEM role models, the Office of Personnel Management issued guidance in August 2012 to all agencies on the flexibilities available to them in support of these efforts, and offered official training for Federal STEM employees on how to effectively engage in these activities. The Department of Energy hosted on February 4, 2014 a first ever STEM Volunteer Fair to provide interested Federal employees with access to programs looking for STEM mentors and volunteers.

Evidence-based Policy to Reduce Barriers to Women in STEM Careers. The National Institutes of Health (NIH) released at the White House Summit on Working Families, a comprehensive summary of research on barriers and opportunities to attract and retain women in biomedical science careers and will use this evidence base to guide Administration policies to broaden participation and success in STEM fields.

U.S. Patent and Trademark Office (USPTO) Reaches Girls to Spark Innovation. In 2013, the USPTO reached more than 3000 girls through targeted programming focused on intellectual property and science, technology, engineering, art, design and mathematics. These programs included workshops on 3D printing, invention concepts, engineering design, product packaging, and patent and trademark protection.

Department of Labor Leads Effort to Provide Pathways for Women to STEM and Other Careers in which they are Underrepresented. U.S. Department of Labor (DOL) released a resource guide on women and minorities in apprenticeships, including tools to help employers and community-based organizations increase the representation of women and minorities in apprenticeships, as well as improve performance and completion rates. DOL developed a digital clearinghouse to share the latest and best information on access to non-traditional occupations, including promising industry practices, job and training opportunities, and relevant research and data for use by trade associations, training organizations, employers, and women interested in non-traditional occupations and apprenticeship opportunities. The U.S. Equal Employment Opportunity Commission (EEOC), DOJ, and DOL remain committed to enforcement of Federal laws requiring equal employment opportunity without regard to gender. Through outreach and technical assistance to foster voluntary compliance, and through enforcement and litigation where necessary, EEOC, DOJ and DOL worked to prevent and remedy discriminatory practices that "steer" women and men into specific jobs based on gender or impose barriers to hiring and advancement that exclude qualified women, and also to prevent and remedy sexual harassment and other practices that can discourage men and women from working in traditionally gender-segregated occupations.

2) Efforts Abroad

(a) Education

Broad Investment. The U.S. Government is committed to improving opportunities for children in low-income countries to receive a quality education and obtain the skills they need to live healthy and productive lives. This includes an average annual investment of $1 billion by USAID in international education efforts to ensure equitable treatment of boys and girls, provide the basic skills that will allow them to succeed and stay in school, create safe school environments, and engage communities in support for girls' education. The U.S. Department of State and U.S. Peace Corps lead global programs to empower girls and increase their chances for academic success, such as through Peace Corps' GLOW (Girls Leading Our World) Camps. The United States' combined efforts extend well beyond traditional classroom activities because there are numerous obstacles to girls education. Focus areas include ensuring girls have equal access to education; helping girls stay healthy and in school; ensuring girls have access to learning in conflict and crisis; and supporting girls' leadership. These efforts include programs to prevent early and forced marriage, initiatives that educate girls about healthy behavior and reproductive health, and efforts to prevent and mitigate the impact of HIV/AIDS.

Policy and Advocacy. The United States Government also engages in several multilateral, global policy and advocacy initiatives that promote girls' education and gender equality in education. In 2014, the United States became one of 14 champion countries for the U.N. Global Education First Initiative, which seeks to raise education to the top of the public and policy agenda by putting every child in school; improving the quality of learning; and fostering global citizenship. USAID is part of the U.N. Girls Education Initiative Technical Advisory Committee and sits on the Board of Directors of the Global Partnership for Education - a global partnership between developing countries, donor governments and public, private, and civil society organizations - to galvanize and coordinate an international effort to deliver a quality education to all girls and boys, prioritizing the poorest and most vulnerable. In addition, USAID launched the Let Girls Learn initiative, through which the United States has broadened awareness of the issue impacting girls' education, promoted opportunities for the pubic to take action, and pledged millions of dollars to new education programs around the world.

(b) Training

Expanding Training for Women. The Department of State and USAID provide training to promote women in leadership across sectors, all around the world. This includes in the health, education, economic, law enforcement, and security sectors. Furthermore, the United States integrates attention to gender equality issues in a broad range of training materials, emphasizing the specific needs and opportunities for women.

Educational Exchange Programs. The Department of State supports student leader institutes in the U.S. for foreign women undergraduates from the developing world; after-school English classes overseas for disadvantaged teenage girls and boys; and training for teachers to strengthen their ability to recognize and address the unique challenges girls face in the classroom. The Empowering Women and Girls through Sports Initiative works to inspire more women and girls to become involved in sports and experience the benefits of participation, such as improved health, increased self-esteem, and greater academic and professional success.

Young African Leaders Initiative. The Mandela Washington Fellowship for Young African Leaders Initiative (YALI) run by the Department of State brings dynamic young African leaders, ages 25-35, from across the continent to the United States for six weeks of leadership training and mentoring at twenty U.S. universities in colleges in three areas: business and entrepreneurship, civic engagement; and public administration. The Fellowship capitalizes on the opportunity to engage and empower a new generation of African leaders to understand and address gender and other inequalities. 500 Fellows were chosen for the 2014 Fellowship, 50 percent of whom were women.

(c) Promoting Opportunities for Women in Science, Technology, Engineering, and Mathematics (STEM)

Harnessing technology and STEM education to promote women's empowerment. The Department of State and USAID are expanding efforts to empower women with technology, including through the GSMA mWomen program, designed to close the gender gap in mobile technology. Agencies, including the Department of Education, are also supporting global efforts to advance women's participation in science, technology, engineering, and math (STEM) fields. For example, the Department of State's TechWomen is designed to enable women to reach their full potential in the tech industry. Women from Africa and the Middle East participate in this peer mentoring program with American women at leading technology and innovation companies in Silicon Valley and the San Francisco Bay Area. A delegation of American Mentors then travel to Rwanda and Morocco to join TechWomen alumnae in conducting outreach programming focused on technology and tech careers for young women and girls. TechGirls offers teenage girls from the Middle East and North Africa the opportunity to participate in an exchange program in the United States that equips them with skills and resources to pursue higher education and careers in technology.

C.   Women and Health

1) Domestic Efforts

(a) Expanding Women's Access to Quality, Affordable Health Care

Preventing Insurance Companies from Denying Coverage or Raising Premiums Based on Gender or Pre-Existing Conditions, Including Pregnancy. The Affordable Care Act (ACA) ensures that every American can access high-quality, affordable coverage, providing health insurance to millions of Americans. More than 4.3 million women and girls enrolled in coverage through the Health Insurance Marketplace in the first historic open enrollment period, and millions more gained coverage through Medicaid. In addition, because of the Affordable Care Act more than 1.1 million women between the ages of 19 and 25 who would have been uninsured gained currently receive health coverage under a parent's health insurance plan and millions more are newly insured through Medicaid or the Health Insurance Marketplaces.

Making Women's Preventive Health Care Affordable, Including Contraception. Thanks to the Affordable Care Act, most insurance plans must cover preventive services including contraception, mammograms, HIV testing and counseling, domestic violence counseling, and testing for gestational diabetes with no deductibles, copayments, or coinsurance. As of June 2014, due to the Affordable Care

Act, 29.7 million women are estimated to have access to expanded preventive services coverage in private insurance plans.

Protecting Women's Access to Reproductive Health Services. President Obama has consistently supported and defended Title X family planning clinics, proposing funding increases for these clinics above prior year levels in each year of his Administration. For many women, a family planning clinic is their entry point into the health care system and is their primary source of care. These services are highly cost-effective, saving $4 for every $1 spent.

Preventing Teen Pregnancy and Supporting Pregnant and Parenting Students. As part of his FY 2015 Budget, the President included $105 million to support community efforts to reduce teen pregnancy. Additionally, $7 million in Public Health Service Act evaluation funding is included for the evaluation of teen pregnancy prevention activities. Teen pregnancy funding will be used for replicating programs that have proven effective through rigorous evaluation to reduce teenage pregnancy; for research and demonstration grants to develop, replicate, refine and test additional models and innovative strategies; and for training, technical assistance, and outreach. In addition, in June 2013, the Department of Education's Office for Civil Rights issued a Dear Colleague Letter and Pamphlet on "Supporting the Academic Success of Pregnant and Parenting Students Under Title IX of the Education Amendments of 1972" (June 25, 2013) to help support pregnant and parenting students.

Improving Maternal and Child Health Outcomes. The Administration launched the Maternal Infant, and Early Childhood Home Visiting (MIECHV) Program, which supports voluntary, evidence-based home visiting programs for at-risk families during pregnancy and children's early years of life in over 700 communities and in all 50 states.

Expanded Health Care and Outreach for Women Veterans and Service Members. With 2.2 million women Veterans in America, VA is working to provide comprehensive health care for women Veterans, including 141 full-time Women Veterans Program Managers at every VA health care system.

(b) Nutrition

Supporting Nutrition for Women, Children and Infants. The President's Budget for fiscal year 2015 includes $6.8 billion to support the 8.7 million individuals expected to participate in the Special Supplemental Nutrition Program for Women, Infants, and Children (WIC), which is critical to the health of pregnant women, new mothers, infants, and young children. The Budget also supports changes to the food package WIC provides that will improve consumption of nutritious foods that are important to healthy child development.

Supporting Mothers Who Choose to Breastfeed. As a result of the Affordable Care Act that President Obama signed into law, many women will now be provided reasonable break times and space at work to express breast milk, up until a child's first birthday. The U.S. Surgeon General also launched a nationwide effort to support mothers who are breastfeeding. In addition, USDA's Supplemental Nutrition Program for Women, Infants and Children (WIC) program has provided nutrition assistance and breastfeeding support to more than two million low-income pregnant, breastfeeding and postpartum women, as well as to their children.

- **Providing Nutrition Assistance and Breastfeeding Support.** USDA's Supplemental Nutrition Program for Women, Infants and Children (WIC) program provided nutrition assistance and breastfeeding support to more than two million low-income pregnant, breastfeeding and postpartum women, as well as to their children. For the first time, the proportion of breastfeeding women exceeded that of non-breastfeeding postpartum women in the WIC program. In addition,

USDA's Supplemental Nutrition Assistance Program (SNAP) lifted nearly 1.4 million households headed by single women out of poverty, including approximately 600,000 households headed by women with children.

- **Promoting Breastfeeding Initiation and Maintenance**. In 2013, HHS launched It's Only Natural, a campaign to promote breastfeeding among African-American mothers. This campaign provides tools, information, and personal stories to help women overcome challenges, find support, and fit breastfeeding into their lives. The campaign has been widely disseminated through print and online media. HHS also operates a national breastfeeding helpline, through which trained breastfeeding peer counselors answer questions and offer support by phone. The helpline provided support to 3,776 mothers and their families over 2013.

Improving School Meals. President Obama strongly supported the passage of the Healthy, Hunger-Free Kids Act of 2010, which included significant reforms to the school lunch and breakfast programs for the first time in over 15 years. The groundbreaking legislation is helping American public schools offer healthier school meals for tens of millions of American children. In January 2012, the Administration released new school meal regulations to boost the quality and nutrition of our national school lunch and breakfast programs — including offering more fruits, vegetables, and whole grains and less sodium, saturated fat, and trans fats. Through the HealthierUS School Challenge, more than 5,000 schools now meet high standards in nutrition and fitness.

(c) Other

Improving Outcomes for Pregnant Women and Infants Affected by Prescription Drug Abuse. The Administration continues to focus on vulnerable populations affected by prescription drug abuse, including pregnant women and their newborns. Research suggests that over the last decade the prevalence of pregnant women using prescription drugs may have increased. In 2012, the Administration held a symposium of key stakeholders and researchers aimed at improving outcomes for opioid dependent women and their newborns. From this symposium, partnerships developed around the country focused on this emerging issue, including partnerships with the National Governor's Association and the Association of State and Territorial Health Officials. The Office of National Drug Control Policy will continue to engage key stakeholders to improve public health systems and outcomes for pregnant women and infants affected by prescription drug abuse.

2) Efforts Abroad

(a) Global Health Initiative

Promoting Gender Integration across all Global Health Efforts. President Obama has placed women, girls, and gender equality at the heart of his global health agenda, including through the Global Health Initiative (GHI). Launched by President Obama in 2009, GHI sets forth an integrated approach to global health, which includes seven core principles, the first of which focuses on women, girls, and gender equality.

(b) Women and HIV/AIDS

PEPFAR. The U.S. President's Emergency Plan for AIDS Relief (PEPFAR) has ensured a comprehensive approach to meeting the HIV prevention, treatment, and care needs of women and girls. PEPFAR's efforts are aimed at providing services, promoting equitable norms, and addressing the gender norms and inequities that play a role in and impact women and men's risk and vulnerability to HIV. More than 4.3 million women currently receive HIV treatment through PEPFAR support and nearly 32 million have been tested for HIV. PEPFAR has boosted efforts to prevent HIV infection for survivors of gender-based (including sexual) violence and to end mother-to-child transmission of HIV. In Fiscal Year 2013, PEPFAR supported testing and counseling for more than 12.8 million pregnant women. For 780,000 of these women who tested positive for HIV, PEPFAR provided antiretroviral medications (ARVs) to prevent mother-to-child transmission (PMTCT). Additionally, in 2013 PEPFAR celebrated the one millionth baby born HIV-free. PEPFAR is also supporting the expansion of lifelong treatment for women living with HIV who are identified as part of PMTCT programs. Over the last four years, PEPFAR spent more than $260 million on GBV programming and gender-related special initiatives, reaching over 114,000 individuals with post-exposure prophylaxis to prevent HIV for sexual violence survivors in 19 countries.

(c) Family Planning

In January 2009, President Obama rescinded the Mexico City Policy which denied federal funds to health care and aid organizations that used non-U.S. government funding to perform or offer information about abortion services. USAID advances and supports voluntary family planning programs in more than 45 countries across the globe. In FY 2013 for example, USAID's family planning programs reached more than 84 million women and averted 21 million unintended pregnancies, preventing 15,000 maternal deaths and saving the lives of more than 230,000 infants. The U.S. Government has also restored funding to the UN Population Fund (UNFPA), providing over $200 million in funding since 2009 to the largest multilateral provider of family planning and reproductive health information and services with programs in 150 countries.

(d) Public-Private Partnerships

The United States has joined with the private sector, foundations, and civil society partners to launch alliances to promote women's and girls' empowerment through global health efforts. The Department of State and USAID are linking health programs to others that address the legal, social and cultural barriers that inhibit women's access to health care, such as gender-based violence, lack of education, and the low social status of women and girls. Examples include:

- o *Saving Lives at Birth: A Grand Challenge for Development*, which is a USAID led global call for groundbreaking, scalable solutions to address infant and maternal mortality around the time of birth.
- o *Saving Mothers, Giving Life*, a USAID-led public-private partnership that has reduced the maternal mortality rate by strengthening country district health systems through health worker training, infrastructure improvements, and linkages to transportation. The partnership has increased the number of births taking place in a health facility; increased the number of facilities offering basic emergency obstetric and newborn services; and expanded testing and treatment for the prevention of mother-to-child transmission of HIV.
- o *Global Alliance for Clean Cookstoves*, a public-private partnership launched with the support of the United States and led by the United Nations Foundation, works to save lives, improve livelihoods, empower women, and protect the environment by creating a thriving global market for clean and efficient household cooking solutions. Today, over four million people a year die because of exposure to smoke from dirty cookstoves – it is the second worst overall health risk factor in the world for women and girls. More efficient and cleaner stoves and fuels can prevent these deaths, improve the wellbeing of millions of women and girls, and empower women economically. The United States has made a $75 million commitment to strengthen and scale adoption of clean cooking solutions worldwide.

o *Mobile Alliance for Maternal Action (MAMA), a public-private partnership founded by USAID, the United Nations Foundation,* delivers health information to new and expectant mothers through mobile phones. Partners include Johnson & Johnson, mHealth Alliance, and BabyCenter.

D.   Violence against Women

1)   Domestic Efforts

(a) Policies and Services

Combating Sexual Assault on College Campuses. On January 22, 2014 the President signed a Presidential Memorandum establishing the White House Task Force to Protect Students from Sexual Assault. On April 29, 2014, the Task Force released its first 90-day report with recommendations and actions focused on helping schools identify the extent of sexual assault on their campuses through climate surveys, developing evidence-based prevention strategies to prevent sexual assault, helping schools to respond effectively when a student is sexually assaulted, providing training for school officials, and improving and making more transparent federal enforcement efforts. As part of the broader effort to combat campus assault, On September 19th, 2014 the President and Vice President launched a campaign called *It's On Us,* encouraging Americans to make a personal commitment to work to change social norms that allow violence to occur. *It's On Us* reminds victims of sexual assault that they are not alone and it is on all Americans to intervene. The Office for Civil Rights at the Department of Education has ramped up enforcement of federal civil rights laws and raised the visibility of federal investigations at colleges and universities. The Department of Justice's (DOJ's) Office on Violence Against Women (OVW) has provided critical grants, training and support to help schools develop comprehensive sexual assault prevention and response programs. DOJ's Civil Rights Division has vigorously enforced civil rights laws prohibiting sex discrimination on campus and in communities, including sexual assault and harassment, resulting in landmark agreements over the last two years that provided robust and comprehensive protections for students from sexual assault and gender biased policing.

Improving the Response to Rape and Sexual Assault. The Obama Administration has developed an unprecedented response to rape and sexual assault. In 2011, the National Institute of Justice developed pilot projects to address the backlog of rape kits in targeted cities. In 2012, the Department of Justice modernized the Federal Bureau of Investigation's (FBI) Uniform Crime Report definition of rape, which will lead to a more comprehensive statistical reporting of rape nationwide. For the first time, rapes of men and boys will be included in our national crime statistics. The old definition- which only covers rape of women by force- did not capture the true impact of this crime. Because the new definition is more inclusive, reported crimes of rape are likely to rise in future years. As Vice President Biden noted at the time: "Rape is a devastating crime and we can't solve it unless we know the full extent of it." President Obama's 2015 budget proposes additional funds to further improve the response to rape and sexual assault by testing more rape kits, developing cold case units to investigate these crimes, and developing trauma-informed law enforcement practices. On April 12, 2013, Attorney General Eric Holder released the updated "National Protocol for Sexual Assault Medical Forensic Examinations, Adult/Adolescent" (SAFE Protocol, 2nd edition). The revised SAFE Protocol uses the latest information and best practices to improve the quality of services victims receive. When followed, the Protocol also improves the quality of forensic evidence collected, enhances law enforcement's ability to collect information and file charges, and increases the likelihood of successful prosecution.

The Violence Against Women Act (VAWA). Authored by then-Senator Biden in 1994, VAWA provides resources for states and local communities to improve the criminal justice response to violence against women and to support victim services. On March 7, 2013, President Obama signed the Violence Against Women Reauthorization Act (VAWA) of 2013, which includes provisions that support the sovereignty of American Indian and Alaska Native tribes and hold perpetrators accountable – a necessary step to reducing violence against Native women. The reauthorization of VAWA also ensures that lesbian, gay, bisexual and transgender survivors have access to the services they need and deserve; protecting victims in publicly subsidized housing from evictions or denials of housing because of the violence they have experienced; and adds protections for college students. Altogether, VAWA authorizes nearly $500 million each year, administered by DOJ's Office on Violence Against Women, to reduce domestic violence and sexual assault.

Addressing the Intersection of Violence and HIV/AIDS. In 2012, President Obama issued a Presidential Memorandum creating the Federal Working Group on HIV/AIDS, Violence Against Women, and Gender-related Health Disparities. Women make up a quarter of the domestic HIV/AIDS epidemic, with Black and Latina women accounting for over three quarters of the new HIV infections annually. Studies show that more than half of all HIV-positive women have experienced violence in their lifetime. In 2013, the interagency federal working group developed a 56-point action plan, with a focus on women of color, to improve screening for intimate partner violence (IPV) and HIV, address violence and trauma among HIV positive women in care, expand HIV and IPV outreach, education, and prevention, and promote increased research around HIV and women/girls.

Leading by Example in the Federal Workplace. Many victims of domestic violence report being harassed at work, and the United States Centers for Disease Control and Prevention (CDC) estimates that domestic violence costs our national economy more than 8 billion dollars a year in lost productivity and health care costs alone. Employers can make a difference by supporting victims and ensuring safe workplaces. To lead by example, President Obama announced new efforts to help combat and prevent domestic violence in the federal workplace. In April 2012, the President directed federal agencies to develop policies to address the effects of domestic violence and provide assistance for employees who may be experiencing domestic violence. These policies will also serve as a model for private sector employers.

Preventing Teen Dating Violence. In 2011, Vice President Biden created the *1 is 2 Many Campaign* to raise awareness about teen dating violence and sexual assault. That same year, the Office on Violence Against Women (OVW) at the Justice Department provided funding for the National Dating Abuse Helpline to use the latest technology to be available around the clock by text, online chat, or phone so that teens and young adults can reach out in the way they feel most comfortable. OVW also provided grants to help middle and high schools address dating violence by training school administrators, faculty, and staff; developing school-wide policies; providing support services; creating effective prevention strategies; and collaborating with local victim service providers. In 2013, the Department of Education sent an important Dear Colleague letter to school districts around the country urging them to address gender-based violence and providing training materials that can help.

Holding the First-Ever Violence Against Young Women Cabinet Meeting. On July 13, 2011, Vice President Biden convened the first ever Cabinet-level meeting to assess progress and discuss next steps in addressing violence against young women. Agencies across the Federal government committed to expanding their efforts to raise public awareness, use technology to reach teens and young adults, and change social norms about abuse.

Funding Culturally Specific Programs. Under the Violence Against Women Act (VAWA), the Department of Justice funds grants to provide culturally specific services in underserved communities. Through these grants, community-based providers partner with domestic violence and sexual assault programs to develop services that are relevant and driven by community needs. Over the past five years, the Department has provided $43 million in grants to develop these services. In 2012, the Department created a priority focus on underserved African American communities, and the Department funds national training and technical assistance efforts through the National Organization of Sisters of Color Ending Sexual Assault and the Institute on Domestic Violence in the African American Community. The Department of Health and Human Services also funds the Institute on Domestic Violence in the African American Community and the National Latin@ Network to advance effective, culturally specific remedies for domestic violence.

Pioneering Approaches to Save Women's Lives. On March 13, 2013, Vice President Biden and Attorney General Holder announced the first-ever Domestic Violence Homicide Prevention Demonstration Initiative grant awards to 12 cities and counties totaling $2.3 million. DOJ's OVW is partnering with the National Institute of Justice to rigorously evaluate the implementation and outcomes of this initiative, which is based on successful homicide reduction models in Massachusetts and Maryland. These models use a short list of screening questions to identify victims who may be in fatally abusive relationships. Once at-risk victims or offenders are identified, law enforcement, prosecution, courts, and service providers can take action to protect victims and their families. This team of responders can search for open warrants, make arrests, connect victims with services, and use pretrial conditions to keep offenders in custody.

Improving Healthcare Responses to Domestic Violence. Under the Affordable Care Act, standard preventive care measures covered under most health plans will now include screening for domestic violence at no additional cost.

Increasing Financial Capability for Victims of Abuse. The Department of Health and Human Services collaborated with the Assets for Independence (AFI) Program to create a comprehensive online toolkit to provide grantees information on the nature of domestic violence and economic abuse, materials for domestic violence service providers to learn about a range of asset building services that can help their clients, and training materials for both communities on how to best help domestic violence survivors access financial services and savings programs.

Eliminating Female Genital Mutilation/Cutting. The United States also addresses Female Genital Mutilation and Cutting (FGM/C) within its own borders, and in 2013, Congress criminalized the knowing transportation of a girl younger than 18 years old outside of the U.S. for the purposes of performing FGM/C (so-called "vacation cutting"). The Department of Health and Human Services funds domestic community-based organizations in populations where girls are most at risk for FGM/C. Recognizing that updated data is needed in order to drive response, in 2014, the Centers for Disease Prevention and Control announced they would produce a report estimating the number of girls at risk for or who have already undergone FGM/C in the United States.

Combatting Human Trafficking in Persons at Home and Abroad: In March 2012, President Obama directed his Cabinet to redouble the Administration's efforts to eliminate human trafficking, which afflicts people around the world and here at home, including millions of women and girls. Building from the strong record of the President's Interagency Task Force to Monitor and Combat Trafficking in Persons and its member agencies, the Administration has announced a series of new commitments to combat human trafficking at home and abroad. These commitments stem from a strategic framework focused on raising public awareness; educating first responders and law enforcement; increased prosecution of traffickers; protecting survivors through comprehensive social services; and partnering with civil society, state and local government, the private sector, and faith-based organizations to maximize resources and outcomes. Key Administration initiatives include Executive Order 13627, which strengthens protections against human trafficking in federal government contracts; the first ever Federal Strategic Action Plan on Services for Victims of Human Trafficking in the United States, to ensure that all victims of human trafficking in the United States are identified and have access to the services they need to recover and to rebuild their lives; and the report of the President's Advisory Council on Faith-based and Neighborhood

Partnerships entitled, "Building Partnerships to Eradicate Modern-Day Slavery," demonstrating the commitment of a distinguished set of civic and religious leaders to strengthen and expand partnerships with government to prevent and combat trafficking.

2) Efforts Abroad:

(a) Strategy

Launching the U.S. Strategy to Prevent and Respond to Gender-based Violence Globally and the accompanying Executive Order. On August 10, 2012, President Obama issued Executive Order 13623 directing departments and agencies to implement the first-ever United States Strategy to Prevent and Respond to Gender-based Violence Globally. The Department of State and USAID have led the United States' work to prevent and respond to gender-based violence (GBV) by ensuring that this issue is integrated in diplomacy and development efforts.

(b) Programs and Initiatives

Departments and agencies fund a broad range of programs to address GBV in countries and regions around the world. This includes support to increase access to medical, psychological, social, legal, and economic support services for survivors. These programs also seek to improve community awareness of the types and consequences of GBV. Departments also train local health, legal, and law enforcement professionals on gathering medical evidence for successful prosecution and conviction of GBV perpetrators. Examples include:

Together for Girls. In September 2009, Together for Girls was launched, bringing together public, private, U.N. and U.S. government agencies, led by PEPFAR, to address sexual violence against children, particularly girls. The partnership focuses on three pillars: conducting CDC Violence Against Children Surveys (VACS) to collect data to document the magnitude and impact of sexual violence; supporting coordinated program actions at the country level with interventions tailored to address sexual violence against children; and leading global advocacy and public awareness efforts to promote evidence-based solutions. VACS have been completed in Swaziland, Tanzania, Zimbabwe, Haiti, Kenya, Malawi, Cambodia and Indonesia and data collection was recently completed in Nigeria. Six more African countries are planning on implementing VACS.

Safe from the Start. The State Department and USAID launched the *Safe from the Start* initiative in September 2013 to increase the capacity of the international humanitarian response system to prevent and respond to GBV from the very onset of an emergency. The initiative includes support to key humanitarian partners train and hire staff and develop innovative programs to protect women and girls in emergencies.

Emergency Assistance to Survivors of Gender-based Violence. Launched in the spring of 2014, the Gender-Based Violence Emergency Response and Protection Initiative is a public-private partnership between the U.S. State Department, Vital Voices, and the Avon Foundation. This Initiative provides urgent assistance to individual survivors of GBV, including harmful traditional practices, as well as individuals under credible threat of imminent attack due to their gender or gender identity. The short-term emergency grants cover urgent needs such as: relocation, medical and psychosocial care, emergency shelter, legal assistance, and other costs. In addition to urgent support for individuals, the Initiative supports integrated training for governments, judiciary and key civil society in implementing laws that address GBV, as well as targeted advocacy programs for civil society groups working to address cultural attitudes and norms around GBV.

Eliminating Female Genital Mutilation/Cutting (FGM/C). The Department of State and USAID fund multiple community-based projects around the world. USAID works toward the abandonment of FGM/C through a multi-sectoral approach of sensitizing groups and adapting social transformation programs through local contexts, supporting programs to bring about eradication in high priority countries, working with religious leaders to delink FGM/C from Islam, and integrating FGM/C into existing programs across all sectors. USAID is also contributing to the start-up of the Nairobi Center of Excellence to improve health care for girls and women suffering from negative consequences of FGM/C and is participating in the FGM/C Donors Working Group. The Department of State launched in 2014 a new program to address FGM/C in Guinea, impacting up to 65,000 girls.

Combatting Trafficking in Persons. See above overview of work in the domestic section. Further efforts in the international context includes the State Department's annual *Trafficking in Persons Report, which* ranks 188 countries and territories – including the United States – on their governments' effectiveness in combating trafficking in persons. The report provides recommendations for how each government can improve its response to this crime and its findings guide U.S. foreign assistance and diplomatic engagement on human trafficking globally. Through partnerships with international and non-governmental organizations the Department of State and USAID administers foreign assistance funds to target all forms of human trafficking using the "3P" paradigm of prevention (including demand reduction), protection of victims, and prosecution of traffickers. The United States promotes the prevention and combating of human trafficking in a number of multilateral forums such as the United Nations, the International Labour Organization (ILO), the Organization of American States (OAS), and the Organization for Security and Cooperation in Europe (OSCE). The United States' anti-trafficking priorities in these fora continue to focus on advancing global efforts to fully implement the Palermo Protocol to combat all forms of human trafficking and ensure strong protections for trafficking victims.

Promoting Gender Equality through PEPFAR Investments. Through the President's Emergency Plan for AIDS Relief (PEPFAR), the United States is working to strengthen health systems and enhance the capacity of countries to prevent and respond to GBV. Over the past four years, PEPFAR has reached over 114,000 individuals with post-exposure prophylaxis (PEP) to prevent HIV for sexual violence survivors in 19 countries.

E.   Women and Armed Conflict

1) Domestic Efforts

Supporting Women in the Military and Women Veterans by Opening Ground Combat Positions to Women. In February 2012, the Department of Defense announced its intention to eliminate the "co-location exclusion" barring women U.S. military service members from being co-located with ground combat units, a change that opened over 13,000 new positions to women soldiers. In January 2013, the Department of Defense (DoD) announced rescission of the 1994 Direct Ground Combat Definition and Assignment Rule prohibiting assignment of women to direct ground combat units below the brigade level, and directed the opening of all remaining closed units and positions consistent with the Joint Chiefs' Guiding Principles by January 1, 2016. The decision opened up about 237,000 positions to women -- 184,000 in combat arms professions and 53,000 assignments that were previously closed to women based on unit type.

2) Efforts Abroad

(a) Strategy

Promoting Women's Participation in Conflict Prevention, Mitigation, and Resolution and Ensuring the Protection of Women and Girls in Crisis and Conflict Environments. Deadly conflicts can be more effectively ended and avoided, and peace can be best sustained, when women are equal partners in all aspects of peace-building and political processes. In 2011, the United States issued the first-ever National Action Plan on Women, Peace, and Security, and President Obama signed Executive Order 13595 directing the Plan's implementation. Together, these documents chart a roadmap for how the United States is working to accelerate and institutionalize efforts to advance women's participation in preventing conflict and keeping peace. They represent a fundamental change in how the U.S. approaches diplomatic, security, and development-based support to women in areas of conflict by ensuring that that gender is fully integrated into efforts regarding peace and political processes, conflict prevention, the protection of civilians, and humanitarian assistance.

(b) Programs and Initiatives

Implementing the U.S. National Action Plan on Women, Peace, and Security. The United States has engaged international partners and civil society organizations across the globe to empower women, men, boys, and girls as equal partners in preventing conflict and building peace. Furthermore, through humanitarian diplomacy and assistance, the United States promotes women's equal access to relief and recovery resources, advocates for their participation in managing those resources, and works to better address the needs of women and girls. Efforts to implement the National Action Plan include the following:

- **Funding Programming in Support of Women, Peace and Security (WPS) Objectives.** From an analysis of funding for Fiscal Year (FY) 2012, USAID's planned spending included over $100 million of programming aligned with the core objectives of the NAP in more than 30 countries. In addition, USAID established a Women, Peace, and Security Incentive Fund designed to catalyze NAP implementation by USAID Missions in priority countries and support learning that can be applied to future programming. The first round of awards, released in 2013 and totaling $5 million, supported programming in Kenya, Papua New Guinea, Sierra Leone, Libya, and the Middle East and North Africa region. The second round of awards, announced in 2014, will support programming in Libya, Yemen, Uganda, Rwanda, and the Democratic Republic of the Congo. These programs were selected for their potential to strengthen prospects for peace and security through the increased empowerment, participation, and protection of women and girls. USAID also launched in 2012 the $2.6 million Global Women's Leadership Fund (GWLF) program to support the participation of women in critical decision-making processes such as peace negotiations, political transition dialogues, and donor conferences. The State Department provides small grants to support local efforts to advance women and girls' participation in peacebuilding and conflict prevention and resolution, including through the Africa-Women Peace and Security Initiative and the Global Women, Peace and Security Initiative.

- **Building Staff Capacity.** USAID's e-learning course, "Gender 101," provides an introduction to USAID's rationale and approach for integrating gender equality and female empowerment within the Agency's work. Over 4,000 technical and program staff have been trained to integrate gender equality and women's empowerment in strategies and projects, including specific information on NAP goals and objectives. Specialized training opportunities for staff have been launched focusing on crisis prevention, response, recovery, and transition that will be offered as part of USAID's regular training going forward. Specialized tools have also been developed, such as the

INL Guide to Gender in the Criminal Justice System, which provides technical guidance to staff to incorporate gender in all areas of criminal justice assistance.

- **Requiring Gender Analysis in Calls for Proposals.** USAID's Office of US Foreign Disaster Assistance (OFDA) and the State Department's Bureau of Population, Refugees, and Migration (PRM) require that its non-governmental organization (NGO) partners include a gender analysis in all project proposals in order to better meet the unique needs of women and girls and identify and mitigate risks posed by gender dynamics.

- **Championing International Efforts to End Gender-based Violence in Conflict.** The United States drafted and negotiated UN Security Council resolutions 1888, 1960, and 2106 on conflict-related sexual violence, which reinforces the Security Council's efforts to prevent such violence, hold perpetrators accountable, engage women in decision making, and enable support and justice to survivors. Building on its endorsement of the September 2013 Declaration of Commitment to End Sexual Violence in Conflict on the margins of the United Nations General Assembly, the U.S. unveiled several new and expanded efforts to support survivors and hold perpetrators accountable.

- **Training Peacekeepers on Preventing and Responding to GBV.** The Department of State works to enhance improve the effectiveness of UN peace operations to protect civilians from violence, including GBV. The U.S. trains peacekeepers to more effectively protect women from GBV and to avoid sexual exploitation and abuse in conflict-affected areas. Additionally, the program provides financial support to the UN Secretariat on projects related to the protection of civilians, the prevention and remediation of GBV, and child protection.

- **New Visa Guidance on Perpetrators of Sexual Violence.** Secretary of State John Kerry issued guidance in February 2014 which specifies that the entry into the United States of perpetrators – including government officials, at any level, acting in their official capacity – of widespread or systematic violence, war crimes, crimes against humanity, or other serious violations of human rights is suspended. Acts that fall within this visa restriction can include rape, sexual assault, sexual slavery, sexual abuse, enforced prostitution, forced pregnancy, forced abortion, enforced sterilization, or any other form of sexual violence of comparable gravity when they occur in certain circumstances, such as when the acts are widespread or systematic, occur during an armed conflict, or are committed using governmental authority.

F.   Women and the Economy

1) Domestic Efforts

(a) Supporting Working Women and Families

Promoting a Comprehensive Working Families Agenda. On June 23rd, 2014, the White House partnered with the Department of Labor (DOL) and the Center for American Progress (CAP) to host the historic White House Summit on Working Families, which built on the President's plan to ensure a better bargain for hardworking Americans by elevating the ongoing national conversation about making today's workplace work for everyone – from working parents struggling to balance the demands of their jobs with the needs of their families, to businesses seeking to attract and retain skilled workers and improve their bottom lines. This summit was conceived of and executed in an attempt to address the set of challenges laid out in sections (b) and (c) above regarding the role of women and workers with families, in the workplace. The goal was and continues to be, to change the culture and political appetite or change in the United States with regards to issues of equal pay, paid leave, paid sick days, childcare, workplace flexibility and women in leadership. In preparation for the Summit, the White House Council on Women and Girls (CWG) held discussions around the country with working families, employers, business and labor leaders, economists, and advocates to seek out new ideas for ensuring fair pay, encouraging more family-friendly workplaces, and improving and strengthening our businesses and our economy as a whole.

Fighting Pay Discrimination. In 2014, President Obama signed an Executive Order prohibiting federal contractors from retaliating against employees who choose to discuss their compensation. He also signed a Presidential Memorandum instructing the Secretary of Labor to establish new regulations requiring federal contractors to submit summary data on compensation paid to their employees to the Department of Labor, including data broken down by sex and race.

In 2010, the President created the National Equal Pay Task Force, which brings together the Equal Employment Opportunity Commission (EEOC), the Department of Justice, the Department of Labor, and the Office of Personnel Management to identify and rectify challenges to gender pay disparities. Since the creation of the Equal Pay Task Force, the EEOC has obtained more than $91.5 million in monetary relief through administrative enforcement for victims of sex-based wage discrimination. The President continues to advocate for the passage of the Paycheck Fairness Act, legislation that gives women additional tools to fight pay discrimination, and of course, the first piece of legislation President Obama signed into law was the Lilly Ledbetter Fair Pay Act, which restored basic protections against pay discrimination.

Giving Working Families a Raise. In 2014, President Obama signed an Executive Order raising the minimum wage to $10.10 for workers on new federal contracts. He also called on Congress to raise the minimum wage for all workers to $10.10, and index this wage to the cost of living. The President's plan would benefit around 28 million workers. More than half of all workers who would benefit from increasing the minimum wage to $10.10 are women. Since the President called on Congress to act in his 2013 State of the Union address, 13 states and the District of Columbia have increased their own minimum wages.

Expanding Workplace Protections to More Families. President Obama signed legislation that made it possible for flight attendants and crewmembers to access FMLA and expanded coverage for military families, and in June of 2014, the DOL announced a Notice of Proposed Rulemaking to amend the definition of a "spouse" under the Family and Medical Leave Act (FMLA) so that eligible employees in legal same-sex marriages will be able to take FMLA leave to care for their spouse or family member, regardless of where they live.

Making Historic Investments to Expand Access to High-Quality Child Care and Early Education. The President has prioritized continuous improvement of the Head Start program, which serves nearly one million children from birth to age 5 each year. Through the American Recovery and Reinvestment Act (ARRA), the President and Congress took important steps to expand Head Start and Early Head Start by adding more than 64,000 slots for these programs. ARRA investments in the Child Care and Development Fund also increased access to child care for an additional 300,000 children and families. In his 2013 State of the Union address, President Obama called on Congress to expand access to high-quality preschool for every child in America, and established a comprehensive early education agenda with a series of new investments to establish a continuum of high-quality early learning for a child—beginning at birth and continuing to age 5. In 2014, the Department of Health and Human Services began this work with a $500 million competitive grant opportunity to support the expansion of Early Head Start and the creation of Early Head Start-Child Care Partnerships and the Department of Education announced a $250 million Preschool Development Grants competition to enhance state preschool programs and expand access to high-quality preschool for four-year-olds in high-need communities to model the President's Preschool for All vision.

Promoting Access to Child Care for Workers in Job Training Programs. DOL will make funds available for technical skill training grants to provide low-wage individuals opportunities to advance in their careers in in-demand industries, with $25 million of the competition focused on addressing barriers to training faced by those with childcare responsibilities. These funds will give more working families a path to secure, higher wage jobs by addressing the significant barriers related to finding and acquiring affordable, high quality child care—including emergency care—while attending skills training programs.

Supporting State Paid Leave Programs. Every one of President Obama's budgets has included a State Paid Leave Fund ($105million in FY15) that would help States with the start-up costs of creating their own paid leave programs. In June of 2014, DOL provided funds for Paid Leave Analysis Grants to fund four states to conduct research and feasibility studies that could support the development or expansion of state paid leave programs. Grant recipients were awarded in September of 2014.

Ensuring Minimum Wage and Overtime Protections for Home and Personal Care Workers. In September 2013, the Administration released a final rule to extend minimum wage and overtime protections to workers who are employed providing in-home care services for the elderly, the ill and individuals with disabilities who had previously not been eligible for these protections. This rule will help ensure that the nearly two million workers in this industry—roughly 90% of whom are women, and a large portion of them women of color—earn fair wages for a hard day's work.

Attracting and Retaining Women and Girls in STEM. Building a pathway to high-paying, high-skilled jobs for women and girls, the Administration has featured competitive preference for inspiring and engaging girls in science, technology, engineering, and mathematics (STEM) through the President's $4.35 billion Race to the Top program, the 2013 Youth Career Connect grants to redesign high schools so that students complete prepared for college and career, and additional education reform programs. Federal agencies have deployed their STEM workforce and have partnered with the private sector to increase mentorship of girls and women in STEM, for example, by DOE forming new partnerships with 100kin10 and US2020 to reach classrooms and mentors, respectively, with their Women @ Energy series profiling women in STEM careers to inspire the next generation of energy scientists and engineers. Supporting and retaining America's female scientists and engineers was a focus of the June 2014 White House Summit on Working Families at which the National Science Foundation (NSF) announced implementation nearly a year ahead of schedule of cost allowance policies for childcare at professional conferences that lessen the challenges for working families and the National Institutes of Health (NIH) released a comprehensive summary of research on barriers and opportunities to attract and retain women in biomedical science careers and is using that evidence base to guide Administration policies to broaden participation and success of women in STEM fields.

Tax Credits for Working Families. Early in his Administration, President Obama pushed for significant improvements to tax credits for working families, which Congress extended on a bipartisan basis through 2017. These improvements include expansions to the Earned Income Tax Credit (EITC) and Child Tax Credit, which strengthen work incentives and help parents afford the costs of raising a family, and the creation of the American Opportunity Tax Credit, which helps working and middle-class families pay for college. Together, these improvements provide an average of more than $1,000 in tax relief to 26 million families every year.

The Federal Government as a Model Employer. To strengthen the government's position as a model employer for working families, in 2014 President Obama signed a Presidential Memorandum to support executive departments and agencies in their efforts to better utilize existing and develop new workplace flexibilities and work-life programs, including enshrining the right to request work schedule flexibilities for Federal employees aware of their right to request work schedule flexibilities. Additionally, in 2010 President Obama signed the Telework Enhancement Act which requires Federal agencies to promote the use of telework. Furthermore, in 2010 the President signed legislation establishing an Office of Minority and Women Inclusion in the Department of Treasury, the Office of the Comptroller of the Currency, the Federal Deposit Insurance Corporation (FDIC), the Federal Housing Finance Agency (FHFA), each of the Federal Reserve Banks, the Federal Reserve Board, the National Credit Union Administration, the Securities and Exchange Commission (SEC), and the Consumer Financial Protection Bureau (CFPB). Each office is responsible for all matters of its agency related to diversity in management, employment and business activities.

Supporting Mothers Who Choose to Breastfeed. As a result of the Affordable Care Act that President Obama signed into law, many women will now be provided reasonable break times and space at work to express breast milk, up until a child's first birthday. The U.S. Surgeon General also launched a nationwide effort to support mothers who are breastfeeding. In addition, USDA's Supplemental Nutrition Program for Women, Infants and Children (WIC) program has provided nutrition assistance and breastfeeding support to more than two million low-income pregnant, breastfeeding and postpartum women, as well as to their children.

New Guidelines on the Pregnancy Discrimination Act. On July 14, 2014, the U.S. Equal Employment Opportunity Commission (EEOC) issued Enforcement Guidance on Pregnancy Discrimination and Related Issues, along with a question and answer document about the guidance and a Fact Sheet for Small Businesses. This is the first comprehensive update of the Commission's guidance on the subject of discrimination against pregnant workers since the 1983 publication of a Compliance Manual chapter on the subject. In addition to addressing the requirements of the Pregnancy Discrimination Act (PDA), the guidance discusses the application of the Americans with Disabilities Act (ADA) as amended in 2008, to individuals who have pregnancy-related disabilities. The guidance sets out the fundamental PDA requirements that an employer may not discriminate against an employee on the basis of pregnancy, childbirth, or related medical conditions; and that women affected by pregnancy, childbirth or related medical conditions must be treated the same as other persons similar in their ability or inability to work.

Empowering Pregnant and Nursing Workers with Better Information About Their Workplace Rights. At the President's direction, DOL released a new online map where working families can learn about the rights of pregnant and nursing workers in each state. The map also allows families to see which states are leading the charge in protecting their rights and which are lagging behind. This live map will continue to reflect any future changes in state and federal policy.

Extending Workplace Protections to All Families Equally. Last year, in *United States v. Windsor*, the Supreme Court struck down Section 3 of the Defense of Marriage Act as unconstitutional. President Obama called the Court's decision a victory for same-sex married couples who have long fought for equal treatment under the law, and he instructed the Cabinet to review all relevant federal statutes to ensure the Court's decision, including its implications for federal benefits and programs, was implemented swiftly and smoothly. In June, the U.S. Department of Justice (DOJ) announced that it has concluded that review. In almost all instances, the government is able to extend benefits to same-sex married couples, regardless of where they live. The DOL also announced a Notice of Proposed Rulemaking to amend the definition of a "spouse" under the Family and Medical Leave Act (FMLA) so that eligible employees in legal same-sex marriages will be able to take FMLA leave to care for their spouse or family member, regardless of where they live. This change will ensure that the FMLA is applied to all families equally, giving spouses in same-sex marriages the same ability as all spouses to fully exercise their rights and responsibilities to their family.

(b) Expanding Opportunities for Women-Owned Businesses

Supporting Women-Owned Businesses. The Small Business Administration's national network of more than 100 Women's Business Centers offer women comprehensive training and counseling to help them start and grow their own small businesses. These centers trained and counseled more than 270,000 entrepreneurs in FY12 and 13, many of them in underserved and economically disadvantaged areas. SBA's Women's Business Centers, Small Business Development Centers, and SCORE chapters counseled and trained over 850,000 women in FY12 and 13.

Increasing Access to Credit for Women Business Owners. The President has expanded Small Business Administration (SBA) loans, which are three to five times more likely to be made to minority- and women-owned businesses than conventional small business loans made by banks. Between January 2009 and December 2013, SBA made 57,831 loans worth $17.2 billion to women-owned businesses. In 2013 alone, SBA made $3.8 billion in capital available to women, a 31% increase since 2009.

Expanding Access to Federal Contracting for Women Business Owners. The Obama Administration has implemented the Women-Owned Small Business Federal Contract program, which helps level the playing field for women-owned small businesses in over 300 industries where women are underrepresented by giving them greater access to Federal contracting opportunities. In FY 2012, SBA awarded $16.2 billion of federal small business eligible contracting dollars to WOSBs. The National Defense Authorization Act of 2013 removed the caps on the contracts that were eligible for this program, and in 2013 SBA worked quickly to implement the cap removal, allowing contracting officers to set aside contracts with higher dollar amounts.

2) Efforts Abroad

(a) Initiatives

Launching New Initiatives to Bolster Women's Economic Empowerment. The Administration has launched several signature regional programs to strengthen women's ability to be able to fully participate in the economy and help spur economic growth worldwide. The Administration also leverages U.S. trade and investment programs to support women in emerging markets. The United States Trade Representative (USTR) is helping countries empower women to participate in the global economy, including through the establishment of Women's Economic Empowerment Working Groups in South and Central Asia, and the Department of Commerce is working to support women-owned businesses in emerging markets including Iraq and Afghanistan. Programs include:

- **Asia Pacific Economic Cooperation (APEC) Women and the Economy Initiative.** APEC—a forum focused on increasing regional integration and economic growth in the Asia Pacific—deals with a range of economic and trade issues inhibiting regional growth and prosperity. Beginning in 2009, the Department of State worked with other APEC economies to elevate and integrate women's economic empowerment into the APEC forum. In 2011, during the U. S. host year, the 21 APEC economies adopted the San Francisco Declaration on Women and the Economy and formalized the APEC Policy Partnership on Women and the Economy (PPWE) to address and make specific policy recommendations to increase women's ability to participate in the economy. Each year the 21 economies collaborate to identify the largest barriers and opportunities to increase women's ability to participate in the economy.

- **Training and Networking for Women Entrepreneurs.** The U.S. has created and expanded regional programs to provide women business owners around the world with the skills, networks and support they need to expand their businesses and become greater forces for economic progress. These include the *Women's Entrepreneurship in the Americas (WEAmericas)*, which - launched by President Obama at the Summit of the Americas in April 2012 - leverages private-public partnerships to encourage inclusive economic growth in the Western Hemisphere by promoting women entrepreneurs and reducing the barriers women often face in starting and growing small and medium enterprises: access to markets, access to capital, skills and capacity building, and leadership. The *Africa Women's Entrepreneurship Program (AWEP)* brings together women entrepreneurs across Sub-Saharan Africa to promote business growth, increase trade both regionally and to U.S. markets, create better business environments, and empower each other to become voices of change in their communities. In 2012 and 2013, the Department of State launched a regional women's entrepreneurship initiative in Central Asia and South Asia, which aim to increase access to finance, markets, information, and training for businesswomen by building regional connectivity.

(b) Public-Private Partnerships

Public-Private Partnerships (PPP) to Support Women's Economic Empowerment. Recognizing that women – especially women-owned small and medium-sized enterprises – are key drivers of economic growth worldwide, major U.S.-based corporations, multilateral institutions, foundations, and governments have also launched multi-million dollar women's economic empowerment initiatives through partnerships with the U.S. government. For example, the Alliance for Artisan Enterprise is an international public and private sector initiative housed at the Aspen Institute, with the goal of increasing market opportunities for and productivity of artisans and to elevate the importance of artisan enterprises.

G.   Women in Power and Decision-Making

1) Domestic Efforts

(a) Appointment of Women Leaders in the Executive Branch

The President has appointed a strong team of leaders, including several women, for example:

Cabinet Level
Sylvia Burwell-Secretary of Health and Human Services (since June 2014) – *previous* role Director of the Office of Management & Budget (April 2013-June 2014)
Maria Contreras-Sweet-Small Business Administration (since 2014)
Sally Jewell - Secretary of Interior (since 2013)
Susan Rice -National Security Advisor (since 2013) - *previous* role Ambassador to the U.N. (2009-2013)
Penny Pritzker -Secretary of Commerce (since 2013)
Kathleen Sebelius - Secretary of Health and Human Services (2009-2014)
Hilda Solis -Secretary of Labor (2009-2013)
Janet Napolitano -Secretary of Homeland Security (2009-2013)
Hillary Clinton -Secretary of State (2009-2012)
Karen Mills – Small Business Administration (2009-2013)
Samantha Power –Ambassador to the U.N. (since 2013)

Sub-Cabinet
Gina McCarthy-Administrator of the EPA (since 2013)

Lisa Jackson – Administrator of the EPA (2009-2013)
Katherine Archuleta- Director of the Office of Personnel Management (since 2013)

The number of women in elected office at the Federal level has steadily grown. Today, women account for 16.8% of 535 seats in the U.S. Congress.

Nancy Pelosi was the first woman to serve as Speaker of the House. From 2007 to 2010, she held the highest position in the House of Representatives, where she presided over a Democratic majority and served as second in the presidential line of succession. She is now minority leader.

(b) Women in Leadership

Highlighting Women Veterans in Federal Government Leadership. The U.S. Office of Personnel Management (OPM) will create the Spotlight on Women Veterans in the Federal Workforce initiative which will consist of webinars and town halls with women veterans in the Federal government. This effort will lift up role models for veterans transitioning out of active duty and for women veterans in the Federal government who wish to take on leadership roles.

Encouraging and Supporting Women Leaders in the Federal Government. Women are underrepresented at the highest levels of Federal government leadership. Improving this disparity is a top priority for President Obama. For example, the Office of Personnel Management (OPM) hosted a Federal Women's Leadership Summit in 2012 to promote women's leadership, and OPM is sponsoring workshops focused on navigating the patterns of implicit bias that have historically kept women from moving into executive positions. Finally, OPM is working to close the retirement savings gender gap (studies have shown that women participate at a lower rate than their male counterparts and usually save less, ultimately inhibiting their long-term savings growth) through the Federal Thrift Savings Program by increasing women's financial literacy through education and awareness initiatives.

Promoting Civic Education and Public Leadership for Girls. As part of the Equal Futures Partnership (described in the "Efforts Abroad" section below) the U.S. advances domestic efforts to promote women's political and economic empowerment, including through encouraging new non-governmental initiatives. The Administration has advanced new efforts to promote girls' leadership and civic education, including sponsoring an "app challenge," hosting a conference on girls' leadership and civic education at the White House with the Department of Education and the Rutgers Center for American Women and Politics (CAWP), and advising on the development of a new initiative at CAWP, Teach a Girl to Lead (TAG) – featuring online resources and a national speakers' bureau.

2) Efforts Abroad

(a) Policies and Initiatives

Building a New Multilateral Partnership on Women's Political and Economic Participation. At the UN General Assembly in September 2012, former Secretary of State Hillary Rodham Clinton and Senior Advisor to the President Valerie Jarrett launched the Equal Futures Partnership on behalf of the United States. The Equal Futures Partnership is an innovative U.S.-led multilateral initiative designed to encourage member countries to empower women economically and politically. Equal Futures partner countries commit to taking actions including legal, regulatory, and policy reforms to ensure women fully participate in public life at the local, regional, and national levels, and that they lead and benefit from inclusive economic growth. The Department of State assisted in expanding membership from 12 to 26 member partner countries, working with them to develop concrete actions that would advance women's economic and political participation. The partnership also has several multilateral stakeholders including UN Women and the World Bank.

Promoting Leadership of Women and Girls. The Department of State and USAID have built on longstanding efforts and launched new programs to promote women's leadership and political participation, including in countries in transition and affected by conflict. In 2011, the Department of State launched the Women in Public Service Project, a partnership between the Woodrow Wilson Center and several U.S. colleges to identify, mentor, and train emerging women public service leaders around the world. Since 2009, USAID has dedicated over $100 million in funding to support women's leadership in peace processes, combating gender-based violence, and in a range of other sectors. USAID partners with the Inter-Parliamentary Union (IPU) to support gender-sensitive parliaments and increase attention amongst parliaments in East and Southern Africa to address gender issues, particularly gender-based violence, and works with the U.S. House of Representatives Democracy Partnership to conduct peer-to-peer exchange programs for female members of parliament from a variety of countries and the U.S. on policy issues such as economic growth and poverty reduction. In addition, Peace Corps Volunteers around the world organize and lead GLOW (Girls Leading Our World) camps to empower young women with leadership skills.

Empowering Vulnerable Women. USAID supports Mobility International-USA's Women's Institute on Leadership and Disability (WILD) program, which brings together women leaders with disabilities from approximately 30 different countries to strengthen leadership skills, create new visions, and build international networks of support for inclusive international development programming.

The Secretary's Award for International Women of Courage. The prestigious Secretary of State's Award for International Women of Courage annually recognizes women around the globe who have shown exceptional courage and leadership in advocating for peace, justice, human rights, gender equality and women's empowerment, often at great personal risk. The State Department hosts each year's awardees for a professional exchange to meet and confer with U.S. leaders. Since 2007, the Department of State has honored 76 women from 49 different countries.

(b) Evidence

Building a Better Knowledge Base. USAID is undertaking the Women in Power (WiP) project to better understand women's political empowerment and leadership. The project is mapping USAID programs self-defined as political empowerment and, through targeted case studies, will attempt to better understand the impact of interventions. The study is also defining and testing a new model to measure women's leadership and power in formal political structures to advance critical thinking and guide future programming around women's political empowerment. USAID is working to integrate gender-sensitive information into systems used to understand conflict and fragility to promote more accurate, comprehensive analysis. For example, data sets for USAID's annual Alert Lists, an internal USG report tracking fragility, political instability, and overall vulnerability to armed conflict worldwide, have been updated to include gender.

H.   Institutional Mechanisms for the Advancement of Women

1) Domestic Efforts

(a) Establishment of the White House Council on Women and Girls

On March 11, 2009, President Obama signed an Executive Order creating the White House Council on Women and Girls (CWG). CWG is comprised of representatives from each Federal agency, as well as the

White House offices, and coordinates efforts across Federal agencies and departments to ensure that the needs of women and girls are taken into account in all programs, policies, and legislation. To aid in implementation of the CWG's mission, the President has created a number of positions, such as the first-ever White House Advisor on Violence Against Women and a Director for Human Rights on Gender at the White House National Security Council staff. For the full text of the Executive Order, see http://www.whitehouse.gov/the_press_office/Executive-Order-Creating-the-White-House-Council-on-Women-and-Girls.

(b) Integrating Gender Across Departments and Agencies

Departments and agencies at the federal level of government that are not primarily dealing with gender equality issues take into account the specific needs of women and girls. At each of the following agencies, designated staffers work to integrate gender equality into their work in the following ways:

- In July 2010, the President established an Office of Minority and Women Inclusion in the Department of Treasury, the Office of the Comptroller of the Currency, the Federal Deposit Insurance Corporation (FDIC), the Federal Housing Finance Agency (FHFA), each of the Federal Reserve Banks, the Federal Reserve Board, the National Credit Union Administration, the Securities and Exchange Commission (SEC), and the Consumer Financial Protection Bureau (CFPB). Each office is responsible for all matters of its agency related to diversity in management, employment and business activities.

- At the Department of Labor, the Women's Bureau develops policies and standards and conducts inquiries to safeguard the interests of working women; to advocate for their equality and economic security for themselves and their families; and to promote quality work environments.

- The Department of Women's Health at the Department of Health and Human Services provides leadership to promote health equity for women and girls through sex/gender-specific approaches.

- The Office on Violence Against Women, a component of the U.S. Department of Justice, works to provide Federal leadership in developing the nation's capacity to reduce violence against women and administer justice for and strengthen services to victims of domestic violence, dating violence, sexual assault, and stalking.

- The Department of Veterans Affairs spearheads the Advisory Committee on Women Veterans. The purpose of the Committee is to advise the Secretary of Veterans Affairs on the needs of women Veterans with respect to health care, rehabilitation, compensation, outreach, and other programs and activities administered by VA designed to meet such needs. The Committee makes recommendations to the Secretary regarding such programs and activities.

- At the Small Business Administration, the Office of Women's Business Ownership works to establish and oversee a network of Women's Business Centers (WBCs) through the United States. Through the management and technical assistance provided by the WBCs, entrepreneurs, especially women who are economically or socially disadvantaged, are offered comprehensive training and counseling on a vast array of topics in many languages to help them start and grow their own businesses.

- The U.S. Equal Employment Opportunity Commission (EEOC) protects women's rights by enforcing Federal laws that make it illegal to discriminate against a job applicant or an employee because of the person's sex (including pregnancy) and other factors. The EEOC provides leadership and guidance to Federal agencies on all aspects of the Federal government's equal employment opportunity program.

- The Department of Education's Office for Civil Rights oversees the implementation of Title IX of the Education Amendments of 1972, which prohibits discrimination on the basis of sex in all education programs or activities that receive Federal financial assistance.

At other departments and agencies, including the Department of Treasury and the Office of the United States Trade Representative among others, designated staffers work to ensure that the interests of women and girls are integrated into the policymaking process and the Council on Women in Girls coordinates this work.

(c) Women and the Judicial Branch

Both of President Obamas appointees to the United States Supreme Court were women – Justices Sonia Sotomayor and Elena Kagan. For the first time in history, women now occupy one-third of the seats on the United States Supreme Court. and almost fifty percent of the judges appointed and confirmed to the lower courts by President Obama are women, the highest proportion of any President (as compared to 22% in the previous administration).

(d) Policies

Creating an Ambassador-at-Large for Global Women's Issues. In 2013, President Obama signed a Presidential Memorandum that will help ensure that advancing the rights of women and girls remains central to U.S. diplomacy and development around the world - and that these efforts will continue to be led by public servants at the highest levels of the United States government. After appointing the United States' first-ever Ambassador-at-Large for Global Women's Issues at the beginning of his Administration, the President signed a Memorandum that ensures that the Ambassador-at-Large reports directly to the Secretary and heads the State Department's Office of Global Women's Issues. In this Memorandum, President Obama also recognized the accomplishments and leadership of the U.S. Agency for International Development (USAID)'s Senior Coordinator for Gender Equality and Women's Empowerment, and established an interagency working group led by the White House National Security Council staff.

Integration of Women's Issues in the National Security Strategy and Quadrennial Development and Diplomacy Review. The Obama Administration has brought an unprecedented focus to bear on promoting equality and advancing the status of women and girls around the world. The 2010 National Security Strategy recognized that "countries are more peaceful and prosperous when women are accorded full and equal rights and opportunity." Following this, the Quadrennial Diplomacy and Development Review (QDDR, 2010) provided a directive to the Department of State and USAID to place women at the center of diplomacy and development efforts – not simply as beneficiaries, but also as agents of peace, reconciliation, development, growth, and stability.

Policy Guidance on Promoting Gender Equality and Women's Empowerment. To operationalize the directive on gender integration in the QDDR, the Department of State and USAID released agency-wide guidance on the effective integration of gender equality in diplomatic and development work. Complimentary in scope, the Department of State's Promoting Gender Equality to Achieve National Security and Foreign Policy Objectives" and USAID's "Gender Equality and Female Empowerment Policy", direct the integration of gender equality and the advancement of the status of women and girls in all policy development, strategic and budget planning, implementation of policies and programs, management and training, and monitoring and evaluation of results.

Investing in Gender Integration with the Full Participation Fund. In March 2013, Secretary Kerry announced the Full Participation Fund, coordinated by the Secretary's Office of Global Women's Issues, to support innovative efforts of Bureaus and Embassies to integrate gender in operations, diplomacy, and development.

Bolstering Agency Policies, Staffing, and Training. From the Department of Justice to the Department of Defense, the Administration has expanded training and created new positions to advance these policies. Agencies, including the Department of State, the Millennium Challenge Corporation, and USAID have issued policy and operational guidance to ensure a comprehensive approach on gender equality and women's empowerment. The Department of State integrates gender assessment requirements and guidelines into strategic planning and budgeting processes and increased training opportunities for Department employees on gender, including the first-ever course on gender equality at the Foreign Service Institute. In 2013, USAID issued a standalone chapter in the Agency's system of policies and procedures that outlines in concrete and detailed terms how USAID operating units must implement the Policy including the appointment of a gender advisor for each operating unit.

(e) Data: Collection, Analysis, and Dissemination of Gender-Disaggregated Data

Since 2009, the U.S. Government has worked to build the evidence base on the benefits of gender equality and the status of women and girls in partnership with fellow U.S. government agencies, multilaterals, foundations, civil society, academia, and the private sector. This data is critical to the design and development of policies and programs.

- **Evidence and Data for Gender Equality (EDGE) Initiative.** Then Secretary of State Hillary Rodham Clinton launched this initiative in 2011 to improve the availability and use of statistics that capture gender gaps in economic activity. Working with international organizations and government statistical agencies, the UN Statistics Division and UN Women will lead and manage the Initiative from 2012-2015, which will include: 1) the development of an online database for a harmonized set of indicators on education, employment, and entrepreneurship, among others, and 2) a set of common, pilot activities in a small number of partner countries to develop protocols and data collection methods for sex-disaggregated data on entrepreneurship and assets, two areas with large data gaps.

- **Women's Empowerment in Agriculture Index.** Feed the Future integrates gender-based analysis into all of its investments and employs an innovative new tool called the Women's Empowerment in Agriculture Index, which measures the empowerment, agency and inclusion of women in the agriculture sector in an effort to identify ways to overcome those obstacles and constraints.

- **Data2X.** In July 2012, Secretary Clinton launched Data2X, a collaboration between the Hewlett Foundation, UN Foundation, and the U.S. government to improve policy and programmatic decisions at the national and global levels through the collection and use of gender data regarding economic participation, political and civic participation including peace and security, and social indicators of well-being. The initiative calls for improved data collection and analysis to guide policy, leverage investments, and drive better outcomes to accelerate and improve development, prosperity, and stability.

I.   Human Rights of Women

1) Efforts Abroad

Promoting Women's Rights across Development Investments. Gender equality and female empowerment are fundamental to the realization of the human rights of women and key to effective and sustainable development outcomes. Although many gender gaps have narrowed over the past two decades, substantial inequalities remain across every development priority worldwide – from political participation to economic inclusion – particularly in low-income and conflict-affected countries and among disadvantaged groups. United States' investments seek to reduce gender disparities in access to, control over and benefit from resources, wealth, opportunities and services - economic, social, political, and cultural; reduce gender-based violence and mitigate its harmful effects on individuals; and increase capability of women and girls to realize their rights, determine their life outcomes, and influence decision-making in households, communities, and societies. These goals are integrated across a broad range of programming, and seek to engage key stakeholders to increase their support for women's rights.

Promoting Women's Rights through the UN. The United States has co-sponsored UN General Assembly and Human Rights Council resolutions that promote women's rights, including focused on such issues as "child, early, and forced marriage," "the girl child," "improvement of the situation of women in rural areas," "violence against women migrant workers," and "women human rights defenders." The United States holds a seat on the Executive Board of the UN Entity for Gender Equality and Women's Empowerment (UN Women). For FY 2013, the United States contributed $7.2 million to UN Women's core budget, in addition support to UNFPA and other UN agencies and offices working to address the needs of women and girls.

2) Domestic Efforts

A number of the items mentioned in other sections directly work to ensure the human rights of American women, including but limited to: the economic agenda, work to prevent and respond to violence against women, and ensuring access to affordable healthcare for women, free from discrimination. Other efforts include:

Repealing Don't Ask, Don't Tell. In 2011, "Don't Ask, Don't Tell" was finally and formally repealed, allowing gay and lesbian service members to serve openly in our nation's armed forces. President Obama signed the repeal into law in December 2010, and in July 2011 the President, the Secretary of Defense, and the Chairman of the Joint Chiefs of Staff certified that the Department of Defense had taken all the steps needed to prepare the military for repeal.

Ending the Legal Defense of the Defense of Marriage Act (DOMA): In February 2011, the President and Attorney General announced that the Department of Justice would no longer defend Section 3 of DOMA against equal protection constitutional challenges brought by same sex couples married under state law. In February 2013, the Department of Justice filed a brief urging the Supreme Court to strike down Section 3 of DOMA and the next month, in March 2013, the Solicitor General argued this position before the Court.

Protecting Women's Civil Rights. The Civil Rights Division at the Department of Justice (DOJ) continued to aggressively enforce the Federal laws protecting the civil rights of women, ensuring equal employment opportunities for women in the workplace, holding accountable perpetrators of sexual assault. In 2013 alone, the Division obtained more than $875,000 dollars in monetary relief and damages for victims of workplace sex discrimination. The Division also reached settlement agreements with the University of Montana and the Missoula, Montana Police Department to ensure that women will be protected from sexual assault and harassment. And in cases such as *United States v. Fields* and *United States v. Alaboudi*, the Division convicted traffickers who preyed on vulnerable young women, using addictive drugs to manipulate and compel their victims to engage in commercial sex.

Protecting the Rights of Young Women of Color. The work of the Department of Justice's Civil Rights Division expanded over the past five years, and has protected the constitutional and statutory rights of women, often young women of color. Among a significant body of work, the Division has used the Fair Housing Act to protect women from severe and pervasive sexual harassment by landlords. These victims are typically low-income women with few housing options who are subjected to repeated sexual advances and/or sexual assault. The Division has also worked to help combat violence against women. For example, after investigating the New Orleans Police Department (NOPD), the Division found that NOPD was failing to properly investigate violence against women. The Division expressed similar concerns about the Puerto Rico Police Department and Maricopa County (AZ) Sheriff's Office.

The Division has also entered into groundbreaking settlements with school districts and police departments to disrupt the school to prison pipeline by addressing racial discrimination in school discipline after finding that black students received far harsher consequences than white students for comparable misbehavior. We know this work has a significant impact on girls of color, because the Department of Education's most recent Civil Rights Data Collection found that nationwide, black girls are suspended at higher rates (12%) than girls of any other race or ethnicity and most boys; American Indian and Native-Alaskan girls (7%) are suspended at higher rates than white boys (6%) or girls (2%).

J.   Women and the Media

1) Domestic Efforts

(a) Using Technology to Strengthen Women's Participation in Democratic Processes

In an effort to encourage the participation of women and girls in the democratic process through technology, the White House has:

- Launched "App Challenges" to encourage the development of mobile applications in areas related to women and girls including Equal Pay and Participation in Government;
- Hosted Twitter Town Halls that allow participants to submit questions to White House officials on series of issues such as Women Veterans and Women's Health; and
- Used video conferencing tools such as Google+ Hangouts to host discussions on policy areas such as education and *Let's Move!* With the First Lady.

(b) The Federal Trade Commission

The Federal Trade Commission is a regulatory government agency that work to prevent business practices that are anticompetitive or deceptive or unfair to consumers; to enhance informed consumer choice and public understanding of the competitive process; and to accomplish this without unduly burdening legitimate business activity. The FTC has a number of actions that have helped ensure key consumer protection settlements that stop false, deceptive or unfair marketing practices for products bought by hundreds of thousands of women. For example:

- Apple, Inc., will provide $32.5 million in refunds to settle an FTC complaint that the company billed consumers for millions of dollars of charges incurred by children in kids' mobile apps without their parents' consent. Under the settlement, Apple also will change its billing practices to make sure it gets express, informed consent from people before charging them for items sold in mobile apps.

- In Operation Failed Resolution, the FTC stopped national marketers that used deceptive advertising claims to peddle fad weight loss products from food additives and skin creams to dietary supplements. The marketers of Sensa, who exhorted consumers to "sprinkle, eat and lose weight," will pay $26.5 million to settle the charges; the FTC will make these funds available for refunds to consumers who bought the product. Other companies charged with making unfounded claims include L'Occitane, which said its skin cream would slim user's bodies; HCG Direct, which marketed an unproven human growth hormone that has been touted by hucksters for 50 years as a weight loss treatment; and LeanSpa, which allegedly promoted acai betty and "colon cleanse" weight loss supplements through fake news sites.
- The FTC charged Down to Earth Designs, Inc., with making deceptive claims about its Diapers product's biodegradability and compostability, among other attributes. The company settled with the FTC, agreeing not to make green claims unless they are true and not misleading, can be adequately.

2) Efforts Abroad

The United States works with the media abroad to increase messaging and dialogue on gender equality issues. This includes through trainings, partnerships, and targeted programs.

Developing Innovative Public Private Partnerships using Media and Engagement for Social Change. USAID has developed three new innovative Public Private Partnerships (PPPs) using multi-media tools such as documentary film, mobile games and short videos along with local grassroots engagement campaigns to promote global gender equality. These three campaigns – Half the Sky, Women and Girls Lead Global, and Girl Rising's Engage Campaign – aim to spur public dialogue; create positive shifts in attitudes and behavior; and nurture institutional policy changes to support gender equality.

USAID's Women's Edition. USAID's *Women's Edition* supports women journalists from influential media houses across the developing world to report on women's health and development. Since 1993, *Women's Edition* has worked in 35 countries with 85 journalists. Journalists provide factual, up-to-date media coverage that reflects women's needs and perspectives. After the widely reported gang-rape of a young medical student in India, a USAID-trained journalist from *The Hindu* (a leading English language newspaper) investigated the status of a 2009 national government notification advising states to establish rape crisis centers. Her widely read story (January 2013) on the lack of action on the advisory contributed to national momentum to demand government action. Shortly after her story, a commission formed in response to the gang-rape added crisis centers to its recommendations and India's government announced a pilot project establishing one-stop rape crisis centers in public hospitals in 100 districts.

Edward R. Murrow Program for Journalists. The U.S. Department of State's Edward R. Murrow Program for Journalists brings more than 100 emerging leaders in the field of journalism from around the world to the U.S. each year to examine journalistic practices in the United States. The program engages young international media professionals in a dialogue with their U.S. counterparts, shares U.S. journalism practices, and creates new professional networks with fellow media professionals from the United States and around the world. Since its inception in 2006, the program has brought more than 1,000 foreign journalists to the United States, including nearly 300 women.

S.A.F.E. Initiative. The Securing Access to Freedom of Expression (S.A.F.E.) Initiative funds centers in Eastern Africa, Eastern Europe, Latin America, and the Middle East to provide trainings on physical and digital security and psychosocial care to journalists and other media professionals working in those regions. Each center makes a concerted effort to include women in all trainings and also deals with the difficult topic of sexual harassment in the workplace during trainings.

Increasing Diversity in the Media Sector in Africa. The State Department's Bureau of Democracy, Human Rights and Labor funds a program to promote women's voices in the Great Lakes media sector and to increase diversity within the media sector in the African Great Lakes Region. The program reinforces the importance of women's involvement in journalism, and increases the general public's access to high-quality quality, gender-sensitive media programming, particularly on issues of women's rights.

K.   Women and the Environment

1) Domestic Efforts

(a) Department of Agriculture

Conducted Educational Programs for Young Women and Girls. The United States Department of Agriculture (USDA) has offered a variety of educational programs aimed at young women and girls including workshops on careers in science; a camp focused on natural resources career paths; an Environmental Leadership Institute; and roundtables to encourage girls to pursue science and agricultural careers.

Awarded Funding to Projects Supporting Female Farmers. USDA has supported a number of initiatives designed to help female farmers including education programs that focus on risk and financial management, crop insurance, marketing and estate planning. Examples include: A $98,959 grant to empower farm women in Iowa to be better farm business partners through networks and by managing and organizing critical information; and a $46,204.00 grant to ensure that 541 women producers in Missouri and Nebraska will increase their knowledge and understanding to make better decisions about crop insurance, marketing, financial management, estate planning and other risk management tools.

(b) Department of Energy (EPA)

Empowering Women in Clean Energy to Lead. The Department of Energy's Office International Affairs continues to grow and strengthen the U.S. Clean Energy Education and Empowerment (C3E) program to advance women in clean energy. The United States is one of nine governments supporting the C3E initiative, a network of national-level actions to increase women's participation in clean energy careers worldwide. The United States is working to close the gender gap with a three-part program including an annual C3E Symposium to build a community of professional women advancing clean energy; annual C3E Awards for mid-career leadership and achievement; and the ongoing engagement of the C3E Ambassadors, a group of distinguished senior professionals who serve as spokespersons and champions. At the 4th Clean Energy Ministerial meeting in New Delhi, the C3E initiative launched C3Enet.org, an online network to connect women around the world.

Promote Women's Entrepreneurship in the Energy Sector. In November 2013, the Department of Energy's Office of Energy Efficiency and Renewable Energy's Small Business Innovation Research Program launched an outreach and education effort to increase the number of women and minority business applicants.

Convening Women on Climate Change, Finance, and Community Engagement. The Department of Energy partnered with the White House in May 2013 to host the White House Leadership Summit on

Women in Climate Change and Energy, convening 150 leaders to discuss engaging diverse audiences in climate change and energy, and bringing more women into careers that tackle these fields. Breakout sessions discussed education, workplace, and community engagement on climate change adaptation, resilience, and mitigation and synergies amongst the participants to collaborate on these issues.

(c) Department of the Interior

Involving Young Women in Environmental Stewardship. Agencies across the Department of Interior have supported and implemented youth programming to provide opportunities for students to learn about America's natural resources. The National Park Service's (NPS) Air Resources Division partnered with Girl Scouts of the USA to provide lessons on science and environmental stewardship, and to date, 1,958 Girl Scouts have logged more than 13,000 volunteer hours in parks across the country. In addition, the Office of Surface Mining, Reclamation and Enforcement/Volunteers in Service to America (OSM/VISTA) teams have placed 238 young professional women (out of about 382 total positions, or 62%) in capacity-building roles with numerous nonprofits in rural mining communities impoverished by environmental degradation.

Documenting and Preserving Women's History in Our National Historic Landmarks. The Department of the Interior has also launched an initiative to identify and preserve important sites associated with women's history in America, including the women's rights movement and the lives and contributions of women who helped shape the country. In order to help develop the next generation of environmental stewards, the Obama Administration recognizes the need to ensure that our public lands are open to and help tell the story of all Americans, regardless of age, gender, or background.

Encouraging Women to Lead Healthier Lives. During 2013, the NPS partnered with GirlTrek, a nonprofit organization with more than 15,000 participants and 300 volunteers that encourages African American women and girls to lead healthy lifestyles. GirlTrek offers a Summer Trek series for women at parks like Yosemite, Great Smoky Mountains, and Shenandoah.

(d) U.S. Environmental Protection Agency

Closing Racial and Ethnic Gaps in Childhood Asthma Rates. Roughly 7 million children (including 3 million girls) are affected by asthma, especially minority children and children with family incomes below poverty level. Asthma rates of African American children are around 16%, while 16.5% of Puerto Rican children suffer from the chronic respiratory disease – more than double the rate of Caucasian children in the U.S. In addition, of the 16 million adults with asthma in the U.S., more than 10 million are women – with asthma deaths nearly twice as prevalent among women, especially among women over 35. In May 2012, the President's Task Force on Environmental Health Risks and Safety Risks to Children released a Coordinated Federal Action Plan to Reduce Racial and Ethnic Asthma Disparities to improve asthma care and health outcomes. In the two years since the launch of the Plan, EPA has supported training for about 16,000 health care providers to equip them to deliver comprehensive asthma care, and partnered with the Ad Council to launch a new social media-based series of public service announcements (in English and Spanish) to help parents, caregivers and youth learn about simple steps they can take in their own homes to eliminate indoor environmental asthma triggers and prevent asthma attacks (www.noattacks.org).

Creating Healthier Indoor Environments in Schools and Childcare Facilities. Of the 3.7 million teachers in elementary and secondary public schools in the U.S., 76% are women, as are nearly 95% of the 2.3 million day care providers – many of whom are of childbearing age. Studies have found that indoor air quality problems in our nation's schools are widespread. EPA has been working since the mid-1990s to provide guidance, outreach, and technical support to states, schools and other childcare settings to promote the adoption of indoor air quality management plans to correct and prevent such problems. Data from the 2012 Centers for Disease Control School Health Policies and Practices Study indicates that nearly half of the school districts in the U.S. are implementing indoor air quality management programs to protect the health of students and staff – the majority of which are based on EPA's Indoor Air Quality Tools for Schools guidance. Since 2012, EPA has been working with national, state and local non-profit organizations to reach the other half of the nation's schools where students and teachers are still learning and working in sub-optimal environments.

Keeping Women Informed About Safe Fish Consumption Choices. In 2004, EPA and the FDA jointly advised women who may become pregnant, pregnant women, nursing mothers, and young children to avoid some types of fish and to eat fish that is low in mercury. EPA is continuing to work with communities that rely heavily on subsistence fishing, in which unhealthy levels of mercury in infants persist. To address this problem, EPA provided more than $5 million dollars during 2012 and 2013 through the Great Lakes Restoration Initiative to fund projects that will reduce mercury exposure in women of childbearing age in the Great Lakes region. In June 2014, EPA and FDA issued a draft update to the 2004 advice, which is currently open for public review and comment.

Educating Female Farm-workers of Childbearing Age About Pesticide Exposure. Farm worker populations in the U.S. are comprised mainly of Spanish-speaking individuals (81%) and approximately 21% of these individuals are women, the vast majority of whom are of childbearing age. Since April 2012, EPA has partnered with the Association of Farmworker Opportunity Programs, a worker advocacy organization, to develop a training curriculum that educates women farm workers of childbearing age about the specific risks associated with pesticide exposure when pregnant, and about steps they can take to avoid exposure. To date, 40 stations in seven states have aired public service announcements related to this project. In 2014, the project will be expanded to include a pesticide safety training curriculum in partnership with the Association of Opportunities Programs for female farm workers who are pregnant or who may become pregnant.

Protecting Women and Families from Exposure to Pests and Pesticides in Schools. Through partnerships and grant programs, EPA is working to create safer, healthier learning environments for children and families through use of school Integrated Pest Management (School IPM). Advancing the adoption of School IPM's commonsense approach to pest management helps create healthier indoor settings with reduced risk from exposure to pests and pesticides (which is particularly important for the health of women and children, who are especially vulnerable to chemical and environmental risks). EPA has committed more than $1.1 million in support of school IPM implementation including assistance agreements focusing on Ohio, Indiana, Wisconsin, Florida, Georgia, Alabama, Louisiana (City of New Orleans), Colorado, Utah, Oregon and Washington State. Since May 2012, more than 2 million K-12 public school students across the nation have benefited from expanded implementation of school IPM, and EPA is currently seeking to award an additional $.06 million for school IPM projects that will affect an additional 2.5 million K-12 public school students.

(e) White House Council on Environmental Quality

Women Leaders in Climate Finance and Investment. In January 2014, the White House hosted the Women Leaders in Climate Finance and Investment event to highlight the pioneering role women leaders in the finance sector are playing to mainstream climate change into finance and investment decisions. This event featured speakers from across the business and policy communities. The discussions revealed some key challenges and unique initiatives associated with mainstreaming climate change into finance. The event also brought to focus the real desire to make a positive social and environmental impact through investment decisions and showed that women are playing an increasingly crucial role to make this happen.

2) Efforts Abroad

Promoting Women's Critical Role in Clean Energy Solutions to Climate Change. The Department of State launched the Partnership on Women's Entrepreneurship in Renewables ("wPOWER") in January 2013. wPOWER aims to empower more than 8,000 women clean energy entrepreneurs across East Africa, Nigeria, and India who will deliver clean energy access to more than 3.5 million people over the next three years. To reach this goal, the United States and its partners provide training, access to clean energy technology inventories, and micro-finance loans to wPOWER participants.

Promoting Education. The Department of Energy's Clean Energy Education and Empowerment Women's Initiative aims to inspire women to pursue studies that will help them participate in the clean energy revolution. At the core of this initiative are university talks offered around the world by women leaders in STEM fields. This partnership features commitments from seven nations in addition to private and non-profit partners.

Expanding the Use of Clean Cookstoves and Fuels to Protect the Health and Wellbeing of Women and Families. The Global Alliance for Clean Cookstoves is a public-private partnership, launched with the support of the United States and led by the United Nations Foundation, working to save lives, improve livelihoods, empower women, and protect the environment by creating a thriving global market for clean and efficient household cooking solutions. Today, over four million people a year die because of exposure to smoke from dirty cookstoves – it is the second worst overall health risk factor in the world for women and girls. More efficient and cleaner stoves and fuels can prevent these deaths, improve the wellbeing of millions of women and girls, and empower women economically. The United States has made a $75 million commitment to strengthen and scale adoption of clean cooking solutions worldwide.

L. The Girl-Child

1) Domestic Efforts

(a) Childcare

Making Historic Investments to Expand Access to High-Quality Child Care and Early Education. The President has prioritized continuous improvement of the Head Start program, which serves nearly one million children from birth to 5 each year. Through the American Recovery and Reinvestment Act (ARRA), the President and Congress took important steps to expand Head Start and Early Head Start by adding more than 64,000 slots for these programs. ARRA investments in the Child Care and Development Fund also increased access to child care for an additional 300,000 children and families. In his 2013 State of the Union address, President Obama called on Congress to expand access to high-quality preschool for every child in America, and established a comprehensive early education agenda with a series of new investments to establish a continuum of high-quality early learning for a child— beginning at birth and continuing to age 5. In 2014, the Department of Health and Human Services began this work with a $500 million competitive grant opportunity to support the expansion of Early Head Start and the creation of Early Head Start-Child Care Partnerships and the Department of Education announced a $250 million Preschool Development Grants competition to enhance state preschool programs and expand access to high-quality preschool for four-year-olds in high-need communities to model the President's Preschool for All vision.

(b) Health

Preventing Teen Pregnancy and Supporting Pregnant and Parenting Students. As part of his FY 2015 Budget, the President included $105 million to support community efforts to reduce teen pregnancy. Additionally, $7 million in Public Health Service Act evaluation funding is included for the evaluation of teen pregnancy prevention activities. Teen pregnancy funding will be used for replicating programs that have proven effective through rigorous evaluation to reduce teenage pregnancy; for research and demonstration grants to develop, replicate, refine and test additional models and innovative strategies; and for training, technical assistance, and outreach. In addition, in June 2013, the Department of Education's Office for Civil Rights issued a Dear Colleague Letter and Pamphlet on "Supporting the Academic Success of Pregnant and Parenting Students Under Title IX of the Education Amendments of 1972" (June 25, 2013) to help support pregnant and parenting students.

Launching a New Campaign to Prevent Drug Use by Teenage Girls. According to a report from the Partnership for a Drug Free America, teenage girls are more likely to perceive benefits from engaging in alcohol or drug abuse than teenage boys. The National Youth Anti-Drug Media Campaign's popular "Above the Influence" (ATI) brand has partnered with MTV, Clear Channel, and *Seventeen* magazine on a national campaign, ATI Unwasted Weekend, that encourages teens to spend their weekends "unwasted" and live above the influence of drinking and drugs. The campaign worked with *Seventeen* magazine to sponsor a national contest, inspiring teen and pre-teen girls to live a drug-free lifestyle by expressing their individuality through fashion.

(c) GBV

*See domestic efforts of the "Violence Against Women" section for comprehensive information

(d) Education

*In addition to the below, see section "Education and Training" section (e) on STEM for information about programs to engage girls in the STEM fields.

Addressing Racial Disparities in School Discipline Policies. Schools should provide pathways to opportunity, yet African American, American Indian and Native Alaskan girls receive out-of-school suspension at higher rates than other girls and most boys, increasing the likelihood that they will become involved in the juvenile justice system. In 2014, the Department of Justice and the Department of Education launched the Supportive School Discipline Initiative to disrupt the "school-to-prison pipeline" and ensure that no child's future is diverted or derailed by school discipline policies.

Providing Educational Stability for Youth in Foster Care. In May 2014, as part of National Foster Care Month, The Department of Education and the Department of Health and Human Services released a letter emphasizing the role Local Educational Agencies (LEAs) play in partnership with child welfare to increase educational stability for children in the foster care system. In any given year, there are approximately 400,000 children in foster care, approximately half of whom are girls. Youth in foster care face unique and compounded challenges, especially when it comes to education—they're are at high-risk of dropping out of school and are unlikely to attend or graduate from college. Ensuring educational stability is a crucial step in helping the most vulnerable among us.

Supporting Pregnant and Parenting Students. According to the Center for American Progress, Latina women are twice as likely, and black women are three times more likely, to experience teen pregnancy than their white peers. In June 2013, the Department of Education's Office for Civil Rights issued a Dear Colleague Letter and Pamphlet on "Supporting the Academic Success of Pregnant and

Parenting Students Under Title IX of the Education Amendments of 1972" (June 25, 2013) to help support pregnant and parenting students. The letter and pamphlet, which were sent to school districts, colleges and universities across the country, contain information on effective strategies to support students who become pregnant or father children as well as guidance on educational institutions' legal obligations under Title IX.

(e) Juvenile Justice

Improving the Juvenile Justice System's Response to Girls. Girls make up the fastest growing segment of the juvenile justice system. The number of girls arrested has grown by 50 percent since 1980; with Native American girls four times more likely, and African American girls three times more likely to be incarcerated than white girls. Supporting the needs of girls in the juvenile justice system means recognizing girls' unique pathways into the system, addressing their specific needs through gendered approaches, and holding systems charged with their care accountable. Through its National Girls Initiative (NGI), the Department of Justice's Office of Juvenile Justice Delinquency and Prevention (OJJDP) is working with girls' alliances and coalitions, the States and national experts to actively address the needs of girls who encounter the juvenile justice system. Through the NGI, OJJDP has hosted educational roundtables across professions to build a strong intergenerational network of advocates and practitioners committed to working on behalf of girls. NGI is also developing a toolkit for State, Tribal, and local organizations wishing to develop a comprehensive program for at-risk and system-involved girls. The toolkit will include national standards for working with girls, including gender-responsive assessment tools, staff training curricula, talking points for raising public awareness, fact sheets for professional and stakeholder groups, and other resources.

2) Efforts Abroad

In addition to the efforts captured in the education section, the United States also works to address gender-based violence experienced by girls, and to promote their leadership.

(a) GBV

*See international efforts of the "Violence Against Women" section for information on programs that also benefit girls.

Together for Girls. In September 2009, the United States became a founding partner of the Together for Girls initiative. This unique partnership brings together public, private, UN and U.S. government agencies to address sexual violence against children, particularly girls. The partnership focuses on three pillars: to conduct national surveys and collect data to document the magnitude and impact of sexual violence; to support coordinated program actions at the country level with interventions tailored to address sexual violence against children; and to lead global advocacy and public awareness efforts to promote evidence-based solutions.

Ending Early and Forced Marriage. Every year, approximately 15 million girls, most of whom live in poor and rural communities, will be married before their 18th birthdays, a fate that often robs them of opportunities for education, threatens their health and traps them into lives of poverty. In 2012, USAID released *Ending Child Marriage and Meeting the Needs of Married Children: The USAID Vision for Action*, which complements numerous USAID policies and strategies and informs USAID efforts to end gender-based violence while strengthening the Agency's commitment to children in adversity, gender equality, female empowerment, and youth development. That same year, then Secretary Clinton announced that the Department would begin requiring mandatory reporting on early and forced marriage rates in annual Country Reports on Human Rights Practice. By strengthening reporting on this issue, the United States signals to countries that early and forced marriage is a threat to women and girls' enjoyment of their human rights.

(b) Education

*See international efforts of the "Education and Training" section.

(c) Promoting Girls' Rights

Promoting Women's Rights in the UN General Assembly (UNGA). During the fall 2013 UNGA, the United States co-sponsored the resolutions on "Child, Early, and Forced Marriage" and "The Girl Child."

Promoting leadership of women and girls. Peace Corps Volunteers around the world organize and lead GLOW (Girls Leading Our World) Camps to empower young women with leadership skills.

III. Data and Statistics

A. National Indicators

Although the United States has not established a core set of national indicators that is used on a regular, standardized basis, there are a number of institutions that are involved collecting gender disaggregated data and relevant initiatives. The role of the national statistical office at the Office of Management and Budget is one of communication, coordination, and collaboration with agencies across the Federal government that are directly responsible for information collection. Through these activities, the national statistical office establishes and upholds Federal information collection standards and guidelines. There is a vast amount of Federal data concerning women. Federal data agencies collect and release new and updated information regularly. The primary points of collection include the below, with examples of specific relevant data sets:

- The United States Census Bureau: www.census.gov
  - Historical Table P-40 (Women's Earnings as Percentage of Men's Earnings by Race and Hispanic Origin) https://www.census.gov/hhes/www/income/data/historical/people/
  - Poverty Table 7: Poverty rates by sex https://www.census.gov/hhes/www/poverty/data/historical/people.html
- The National Center for Education Statistics www.nces.ed.gov
  - High school graduation rates by gender and state. http://nces.ed.gov/fastfacts/display.asp?id=27
- The National Science Foundation www.nsf.gov
  - Science and Engineering Indicators: Elementary, Secondary, and Higher Education Math and Science Statistics; Science and Engineering Labor Force Gender Data http://www.nsf.gov/statistics/seind/
- The Bureau of Labor Statistics www.bls.gov
  - Women's Bureau, Latest Annual Data (labor force participation, mothers in the labor force, unemployment, full and part-time employment, earnings, industries, and education). http://www.dol.gov/wb/stats/recentfacts.htm#rates
- The Center for Disease Control www.cdc.gov/nchs
  - Insurance rates by gender and type of coverage http://www.cdc.gov/nchs/data/nhis/earlyrelease/insur201409.pdf
- The Bureau of Justice Statistics www.bjs.ojp.usdoj.gov
  - Latest data "Nonfatal Domestic Violence, 2003-2012" http://www.bjs.gov/index.cfm?ty=pbdetail&iid=4984

In an effort to create a comprehensive look at a set of gender indicators, in March of 2011 the Council on Women and Girls, the Office of Management and Budget and the Economics and Statistics Administration within the Department of Commerce worked together to create the **Women in America (pdf)** report which, for the first time in recent history, pulled together information from across the Federal statistical agencies to compile baseline information on how women are faring in the United States today and how these trends have changed over time. The report provides a statistical portrait showing how women's lives are changing in five critical areas:

- People, Families, and Income
- Education
- Employment
- Health
- Crime and Violence

By bringing together data from across the Federal government, the report is one of most comprehensive sources for information on women's lives today. This is the first such federal initiative since 1963, when the Commission on Status of Women, established by President Kennedy and chaired by Eleanor Roosevelt, produced a report on the conditions of women. The initiative furthers three governance themes of the Obama Administration: (1) pursuing evidence-based policymaking; (2) catalyzing the private sector, including private researchers, to partner with the government in analyzing data and formulating appropriate policies; and (3) pursuing an all-government and all-agency approach to addressing special issues affecting Americans.

In addition to long-running data sources, supplements and expansions to existing surveys provide a more detailed examination into how individuals, including women, are faring. For example, the 2011 supplement to the American Time Use Survey (ATUS), a survey conducted annually by the Bureau of Labor Statistics, enquired about whether respondents had access to paid or unpaid leave or flexible work arrangements. This information was used to inform Administration analyses in proposals and policies affecting working families for the 2014 Working Families Summit.

B.   Minimum Set of Gender Indicators

These indicators, in the domestic context, are integrated in the mechanisms identified above, in section (a).

Around the world, the United States is working to improve the collection, analysis, and use of data and research to strengthen gender equality efforts. Among its achievements, the Department of State and USAID have improved tracking and evaluation of gender activities, including through their performance and budgetary tracking mechanisms. Furthermore, they have supported partners in increasing available data, such as through the USAID-funded flagship Demographic and Health Surveys Program, which has collected, analyzed, and disseminated data on population, health, HIV, and nutrition – with attention to women's experiences - through more than 300 surveys in over 90 countries.

C.   Nine Indicators on Violence Against Women

Most of these indicators, in the domestic context, are integrated in the mechanisms identified above, in section (a).

Around the world, the United States is working to improve the collection, analysis, and use of data and research to improve GBV prevention and response efforts abroad. Among its achievements, the Department of State and USAID have improved tracking and evaluation of GBV activities. In 2011, State and USAID ensured that their performance and budgetary tracking mechanisms include attention to GBV. In addition, the USAID-funded Demographic and Health Surveys Program has collected, analyzed, and disseminated data on the prevalence of emotional, physical, and sexual violence around the world, including through GBV-related questions in the core DHS module, and through a stand-alone Domestic Violence module that some countries choose to include.

Furthermore, the United States has worked to strengthen the capacity of partner governments and local organizations to improve their data collection, research, and analysis of GBV trends. Key examples include work through the Together for Girls Partnership to strengthen systems in Afghanistan, Timor-Leste, Botswana, Costa Rica, and various countries in Sub-Saharan Africa.

## D.	Data on Vulnerable Groups

Each of the Federal statistical agencies listed above also provides data on the situation of women by characteristics such as race and ethnic group; urban status; family situation and living arrangement; age; and state of residence. These data are reported regularly by the statistical agencies, and microdata are also available to the public and researchers who wish to examine specific sub-groups in greater detail.

Examples of specific data collected include:

- **Census:** Historical Table P-38 (full-time, year-round workers by median earnings, sex, and race and ethnic group) https://www.census.gov/hhes/www/income/data/historical/people/

NCES:

- Postsecondary degrees conferred by level of degree, race/ethnicity, and gender. http://nces.ed.gov/fastfacts/display.asp?id=72
- Postsecondary enrollment rates by race/ethnicity and gender. http://nces.ed.gov/fastfacts/display.asp?id=98

IV.   Emerging Priorities

A.   Priorities for Next Three-to-Five Years

From a domestic perspective the United States will continue to ensure a coordinated Federal response to issues that particularly impact the lives of women and girls and to ensure that Federal programs and policies address and take into account the distinctive concerns of women and girls, including women of color and those with disabilities. We will continue to focus on many of the priorities that have guided our work from the beginning of the Obama Administration and set new goals and targets to ensure we are doing all we can to empower women and girls in America. Priorities include initiatives such as:

- *Women in the Workplace/Working Families Issues*
  - Closing the gender wage gap, including the Administration's support of the Paycheck Fairness Act.
  - Eliminating pregnancy discrimination through strong enforcement of existing laws and passage of new laws, such as the Administration's support of the Pregnant Worker's Fairness Act.
  - Supporting paid family and sick leave, including through helping states with the start-up costs of starting their own paid family leave programs.
  - Ensuring and investing in access to quality, affordable childcare and early childhood education.
  - Working with companies to create more flexible and predictable work environments.
  - Raising the minimum wage across the country, including the president's proposal to raise it to $10.10.

- *Women's Health*
  - Implementing the Affordable Care Act.
  - Connecting women to preventive health care services.

- *Attracting Women and Girls to, and Retaining them in, the STEM Fields*
  - Transforming STEM classroom teaching to engage students in real-world problems that inspire girls in STEM subjects.
  - Engaging in a campaign to increase the number of positive images of women in STEM to inspire young girls and women in these fields.
  - Focusing on gender balance in the growing fields of computer science and engineering, in which women and girls currently underrepresented.
  - Addressing structural, conscious, and unconscious biases that deter women from pursuing successful careers in STEM.

- *Preventing and Responding to Violence Against Women*
  - Continuing focus on reducing the incidence of sexual assault on college campuses through policy, enforcement, and public-private partnerships, and expanding this effort to include K-12 schools.
  - Continue to effectively implement the Violence Against Women Act with a focus on underserved communities and new protections for Native American women and LGBT survivors.
  - Exploring new civil rights remedies to address domestic violence and sexual assault.
  - Improving the criminal justice response to sexual assault including addressing the backlog of rape kits and supporting survivors.

- Addressing family homelessness and improving housing options for domestic violence survivors.
- Improving screening rates for IPV in the health care setting.
- Continuing to push our anti-trafficking agenda, with an emphasis in the near-term on identifying meaningful and innovative ways to eliminate trafficking in global supply chains, expanding the use of cutting-edge technology to better direct law enforcement resources, and continue efforts to more effectively link victims to comprehensive services.

- *Helping Women Start and Grow Their Own Businesses*
  - Helping women business owners better access capital.
  - Expanding contracting opportunities.
  - Bolstering high-growth entrepreneurship.

From an international perspective, the United States will continue to promote gender equality and advance the status of women and girls. Informed by a suite of policies and guidance, the United States is working to reduce gender disparities in access to, control over and benefit from resources, wealth, opportunities and services – economic, social, political, and cultural; reduce gender-based violence and mitigate its harmful effects on individuals and communities; and increase capability of women and girls to realize their rights, determine their life outcomes, and influence decision-making in households, communities, and societies. Priorities include:

- *Advancing Women's Economic Empowerment*
  - Continuing efforts in a range of multilateral forums to advance women's economic empowerment and help spur economic growth worldwide, including in the G20, the Asia Pacific Economic Cooperation (APEC) forum, and through the Equal Futures Partnership.
  - Expanding regional programs, including the APEC Women and the Economy initiative, the Women's Entrepreneurship in the Americas (WEAmericas) initiative, and the African Women's Entrepreneurship Program (AWEP).
  - Advancing food security worldwide through the Feed the Future Initiative, with a priority focus on women agricultural producers as critical drivers of economic growth.

- *Promoting the Health of Women and Families*
  - Advancing the health of women, girls, and families through the Global Health Initiative (GHI).
  - Ensuring a comprehensive approach to gender issues in HIV prevention, treatment, and care.
  - Supporting voluntary family planning programs across the globe.

- *Empowering Women as Equal Partners in Preventing Conflict and Building Peace*
  - Implementing the United States National Action Plan on Women, Peace, and Security, including through close collaboration with partners, from the U.N. to local women peacebuilders and gender advocates.
  - Expanding the Safe from the Start initiative to better address the needs of women and girls and other groups at risk of GBV in emergencies.

- *Addressing Gender-based Violence*

- o Implementing the United States Strategy to Prevent and Respond to Gender-based Violence Globally, including by promoting increased access to services, as well as investment in prevention efforts and accountability opportunities
- o Engaging men and boys as allies in changing social norms and preventing gender-based violence.
- o Continuing work on ending child, early and forced marriage and meeting the needs of married children.

- *Promoting Women's Political Participation*
  - o Expanding the U.S.-launched Equal Futures Partnership to break down barriers to women's political and economic empowerment.
  - o Increasing the capability of women to realize their rights and influence decision-making in their communities.

- *Promoting Girls' Education*
  - o Ensuring equal access to quality education at all levels, including in crisis and conflict environments.
  - o Providing the basic skills - like literacy - that will allow girls to succeed and stay in school.
  - o Creating safe school environments and infrastructure including classrooms, bathroom facilities, and routes to school.
  - o Engaging communities in support for girls' education.
  - o Improving workforce development programs to produce a female labor force with relevant skills to support country development goals.

B.   Post-2015 Priorities and Recommendations

The United States strongly supports a stand-alone goal on gender equality and women's and girls' empowerment in the Post-2015 Development Agenda. The United States also supports mainstreaming of gender into all relevant Sustainable Development Goals, as gender inequalities continue to contribute to slow and uneven development progress globally. In addition, the United States recognizes that progress for women and girls will be possible only by including gender-sensitive indicators and requiring the collection of sex and age disaggregated data across all goals and targets. Priority areas include: 1) prevention and response to gender-based violence; 2) advancing women's economic empowerment; 3) promoting women's public and private leadership; and 4) improving universal access to sexual and reproductive health services and promoting women's reproductive rights.